T0146430

ADVANCED-LEVEL AND FRESHMAN ECONOMICS WITH MODEL ANSWERS

Kaela B. Mulenga and Francis L. Mupakati

ADVANCED-LEVEL AND FRESHMAN ECONOMICS WITH MODEL ANSWERS

Book Cover designed by Margareta Oskarsson (Kicki), Solna/Stockholm – Sweden

Copyright © 2018 Kaela B. Mulenga and Francis L. Mupakati.

All rights reserved. No part of this book may be used or reproduced by any means, graphic, electronic, or mechanical, including photocopying, recording, taping or by any information storage retrieval system without the written permission of the author except in the case of brief quotations embodied in critical articles and reviews.

iUniverse books may be ordered through booksellers or by contacting:

iUniverse
1663 Liberty Drive
Bloomington, IN 47403
www.iuniverse.com
1-800-Authors (1-800-288-4677)

Because of the dynamic nature of the Internet, any web addresses or links contained in this book may have changed since publication and may no longer be valid. The views expressed in this work are solely those of the authors and do not necessarily reflect the views of the publisher, and the publisher hereby disclaims any responsibility for them.

Any people depicted in stock imagery provided by Getty Images are models, and such images are being used for illustrative purposes only.
Certain stock imagery © Getty Images.

ISBN: 978-1-5320-5083-1 (sc)
ISBN: 978-1-5320-5082-4 (e)

Library of Congress Control Number: 2018910116

Print information available on the last page.

iUniverse rev. date: 09/22/2018

DEDICATION

--- To Francis L Mupakati who sadly passed on before seeing this book published and witnessing the end of Robert G. Mugabe's era of control in Zimbabwe.
--- To the late Luke Chileshe Mulenga, the poet, my brother and spiritual mentor up to today.

CONTENTS

CONTENTS

FOREWORD

Mupakati the Muntu

Now that he is gone. Oh! Now that my friend Francis L. Mupukati, so youthful and gentle in nature is gone, I can sing to his intellectual accomplishments. But to what avail? Now that he is gone.

Let me praise him and dance to our friendship for his intellectual accomplishments are self-evident. For as providence would have it, we met at a time, when things were unravelling in both of our lives. Thus, we met as spurned, damaged goods that had been flung onto the barbed wired web spun by the cruel invisible hand of the market place. Seeking refuge at a Salvation Army shelter on St. George McCaul; synchronicity introduced us as friends.

~~~

Reflecting on the miracle of being Human in general and on the humanity of Mupakati as a Muntu in particular;

"*Mutual Aid*" the book by Peter Kropotkin comes to mind. Beginning with an analysis of "mutual aid" as a factor of evolution in Nature, Kropotkin brings into question the Darwinian model of economic man as a rapacious groping animal bent upon the accumulation of naked power as a means to display the vulgar acquisition of flagrant opulence.

On the contrary, Kropotkin asserts that so called primitive pre-colonial societies were organized around mutual co-operative economic principles and from the standpoint of societies and fabrics of cultures that find
~~~

themselves on the outskirts of History, it follows that Humans, when untainted by civilization are naturally pre-disposed towards helping one another.

But even more so in his discourse on the pre-colonial social economic models of the Koisan and Bantu Peoples of Southern Africa, Kropotkin is led to the conclusion that these so-called primitive "Peoples Economic" models with their emphasis on the nurturing of the inner man, the Ki or Muntu, one finds the vanguard of the evolutionary march from ape man to the miracle of being Human.

~~~

"You know Pfaff" Mupakati said after we had become room mates; "I was hardly fourteen when I saw a tarred road for the first time in my life." I couldn't believe what I was hearing nor could my imagination envisage what I was being told. For although I knew that he had managed to win a scholarship to go to the University of Cambridge, I just couldn't for the life of me fathom how he had managed to do so, if school life for him began outdoors in classes held under a shaded tree.

Priding myself as a scholar of socio-economic political philosophy, everything and all I knew on the subject matter was reduced to rubbish by this revelation on Mupakati's peasant upbringing, until I remembered that the ancient Greek philosophers gathered their students under shaded trees; not the Parthenon.

There were a dozen of them or so, the brightest young minds from the now independent Zimbabwe attending with full scholarship the University of Cambridge, when President Mugabe paid them a visit and demanded of them what they were doing here at an elite imperialistic University. Pointing fingers and scolding them, the great man insisted that they should all return home and serve the Zimbabwe that he had liberated from Imperialism. They did; only to find themselves sitting around in empty offices twirling their thumbs with nothing to do.
~~~

But more insolently, if not deviously so, most of the millions that both Britain and Canada had provided in scholarship funds for post-independent Zimbabwe were unceremoniously returned by Mugabe. If you wonder how this strange action on Mugabe's behalf can be true, then rest assured it came unsurprisingly right on cue. For as Frantz Fanon in his book "*The Wretched of the Earth*" had maintained; that invariably with post-colonial independence comes the suppression of the education of the broad masses. For only through the cultivation of the mass ignorance of the broad masses, can the new ruling elite entrench and sustain their hold on power; Fanon had insisted.

Confronted with the halting gestures of a whitened sepulchered hand painting to leprous fingers towards the sons and daughters of the ruling elite; the ever imaginative Mupakati found a way around the unholy spectre. Walking thus into the Canadian Embassy, Mupakati demanded as only he could, whether the Embassy staff were incompetent or not, and if not, then why not was his name with his exceptional academic record not on the scholarship list of those whom had applied to study in Canada.

Graciously the Canadian authorities conceded to his just appeals to uphold human rights, despite the devious interventions of the Mugabe Regime to suppress all scholarships that were not intended for the sons and daughters of the ruling elite. Armed thus with a Canadian scholarship, Mupakati headed for the University of Lakehead where he completed his Masters thanks to the generosity of the Canadian government on behalf of the Canadian People.

Exiled from his beloved country Zimbabwe, Mupakati entered the financial field upon graduation, where he had a very successful career as a consulting analyst for a number of years. However, being independently minded and aware of his dependency as a wage slave, he eventually founded his own company which is still a prosperous going concern, despite his untimely passing.

~~~

Not as an actuary, but as an acute observer of the laws of probability, Mupakati had entered into the field of games of chance. There to the consternation of the custodian statisticians overseeing the games of chance,
~~~

Mupakati's name kept cropping up as a lottery winner. Not necessarily a bad thing, but the consistency and regularity with which his name kept cropping up were breaking all odds in an alarming fashion.

Thus, given that upon average his winnings at games of chance were approaching a hundred thousand dollars a year, which, in itself was negligible compared to the millions in lottery jackpots that were being paid out each week. What was the consternation about? Precisely because the manner in which his winnings were being accumulated were defying the *laws of probability* and that was impermissible.

For although he had never won the jackpot where everyone had a negligible, but even permissible chance of winning; the thing that was causing the consternation amongst the custodian statisticians was the fact that the small ones that he was continuously winning in consecutive rows were impermissible by pure chance. In fact, he was breaking not negligible, but infinitesimal odds and that by definition was impossible.

Indeed impossible was the consensus amongst the custodial statisticians and they demanded a legal investigation into Mupakati's winnings. "How could he beat such odds?" they insisted. "There must be some foul play behind his consecutive winnings" they persisted. None was found. Only the disbelief that this educated *African peasant* had defied the "Laws of Probability" and had indeed defied their smug arrogant attitude and that they were going to get Mupakati!

~~~

Mupakati wanted to teach me his system of deviation but I was unwilling or maybe too ignorant to learn. No regrets, but herein lies the tragedy and irony of Mupakati's early departure.

For although he had mastered the art of beating the odds when it came to the game of chance of winning at the lotteries, when it came to the game of life as the Furies would have it when the gods of Luck rolled the dice for the chances of being struck by terminal cancer, Mupakati stood no chance of beating the odds.
~~~

It struck him like lightning and nothing could be done to save him, except to wonder whether his early passing was due to a capricious act of God or as Barry Lynes in "*The Cancer Cure that Worked*" tells us, due to the economic evil acts of men.

But be that as it may. Only time will tell whether we turn this planet we call home into heaven or hell. However, wherever in space-time Mupakati now resides, surely he would be pleased to see this new and expanded edition of "*Focus Study Aids*" released.

Pedro Daniel Pfaff
Toronto, Canada
December 2017

PREFACE

This book was first published as '***FOCUS Study Aids***' to provide model answers for students preparing to take A-level exams. A set of model answers was prepared and tested in a tutorial-type of set-up. In general, the subject matter of most Commonwealth syllabuses was covered in the text.

The main purpose of this *Second Edition* is to revise and update the material. Several new sections have been added to expand or cover recent developments in economic theory. As before, mathematical complexities and relationships are avoided.

However, every effort has been made to explain the theories and/or concepts as concisely as possible using graphical illustrations. The goal is to provide a good understanding of basic economic principles. As such the book will benefit those studying for A-level Economics or Freshman Economics at universities/colleges/business schools as well as those studying for various professional examinations where some working knowledge of economics is required.

Anyone who is looking for an introductory foundation in Economics will find this book useful. Non-student users such as business executives or entrepreneurs seeking a basic understanding of Economics will also find the book useful.

Basic economic concepts and theories, clearly communicated through *essay-type* model answers, are provided to assist students in getting a firm command of the fundamentals of this field of social science.

As a disclaimer, we wish to point out that this book covers only basic introductory economic concepts. A deeper understanding of topics in economics must be sought from more advanced texts.

Kaela B Mulenga
Francis L Mupakati

ACKNOWLEDGEMENTS

It is not possible to name everyone who encouraged or assisted us in getting the manuscript off the ground. However, we would like to thank our former students at various institutions where we have taught, among them: University of Zimbabwe, the University of Zambia, and at institutions in the USA and Canada.

Miss Karen Woychyshyn of Lakehead University, Ontario, Canada typed the first manuscript. Angela Jones of Startnet Print & Copy of Toronto for organizing and re-typing the edited manuscript. Thanks also to Margareta Oskarsson (Kicki), Solna/Stockholm, Sweden, for designing the new book cover.

Mohamed Abdulla, Francis Mupakati's close friend gave lots of business advice and moral support. Pedro Daniel Pfaff, who is known to both authors, provided valuable inputs. Dr. Lois Pineau and Stephen Hwang, TO, for support.

Several friends, family members – the Cliff Mulenga's in Atlanta, Georgia, and acquaintances provided much appreciated emotional support.

We also benefited from comments and suggestions on an earlier draft from Mr. Lovermore Moyo. Chola Mukanga of the *Zambian Economist* also offered useful suggestions on economic theories foundations.

We would like to thank Trevor Millet of Brooklyn, NY, who at the last moment, accepted to go through the manuscript. He made a valuable contribution.

We are also indebted to the team at iUniverse publishing, especially Jacky Aba, and Robin Sawyer, for guidance and encouragement in making this book a reality.

However, any errors or omissions in this book are entirely the authors' final responsibility.

***

INTRODUCTION

In most of the images of rural Africa, you often see mud huts with malnourished children running around. Pictures focusing on urban centers depict school buildings with broken windows. Many of the roads are unpaved and full of potholes.

These general conditions of deficient economic development are prevalent in most Sub-Saharan African countries. Even in South Africa, a country whose economy is fairly advanced, the majority of people—blacks—live in compounds with poor housing and inadequate sanitation. The quality of life of these people is deemed poor due to the critical shortage of necessary amenities of life, such as food supplies and drinking water. Consequently, people's health is generally poor.

A sharp contrast to this is the living conditions of people in economically advanced countries in the West. The necessities of life are available in abundance, and hence, the quality of life and standard of living of a majority of the population is high.

At first, this abnormal imbalance appears puzzling. After careful scrutiny, however, we find that the explanation lies in one word—***"choice."*** Economics is known as "***the science of choice,***" because economists are preoccupied with choice.

Given that we live in a world of *limited resources*—at all points of time, wherever you happen to be, either individually and/or as a group (society)—we all must choose between *two* or *more* competing alternatives. If these choices are made in a rational way, we ought to end up with the *best choice*. In light of the above, if you want to better your life, you must choose the *best* (**optimal**) of the two alternatives presented to you.

As you can see, either as individuals or as a society, our choices can affect our destiny. Regardless of whether we are rich or poor, as long as we are functioning normal human beings, we have the capacity to make choices by employing the resources at our disposal. The choices we make determine where we end up. Taking into account the above, immigration, free trade, climatic changes, poverty, technology transfer, and hunger can all be explained through the process of choice-making.

For example, corrupt bureaucrats deprive their poor countries of the resources that could instead be employed for their all-round development. If people decide not to work on their fields, hunger may affect them down the road. Tribal people, who deny their children from going to school, must be prepared to face the consequences of ignorance.

This book will help you understand the logic economists use and the educated assumptions they make when conducting economic analyses pertaining to the situations prevalent in the real world. You will find *Model Answers* in carefully arranged chapters addressing a wide range of topics. The roles of banks, free trade, inflation, and price fluctuations are among the subjects we have tackled.

The book is easy to comprehend and can, in fact, be read by anyone with high school education.

The glossary at the end of the book provides useful clarifications with respect to the economic jargon. In today's fast-paced digital information age, one must possess the tools to make sense of what's happening. The glossary will be helpful also because economic journals, magazines, business bulletins, or even simple newspaper magazines are oftentimes written in technical language that is difficult for the layman to follow.

We are certain that, by the time you finish reading this book, you will have a fair amount of knowledge with regard to economics. This will equip you with the confidence to participate in well-informed debates on the same. You will enjoy the read!

~~ ~~

Kaela B Mulenga
Toronto, Canada

1 Introductory Concepts and Ideas

General Remarks

Some people think of economics as a dismal science – in that its theories are sometimes not only wrong but they actually predict doom. While theories can explicitly explain how profits are made, they are not concerned about the morality and ethics of obtaining huge profits. And by themselves, these theories do not set universal limits for the maximization of profits or the exploitation of resources.

In the end, some argue that those with financial muscle can take advantage of those with none. Hence, exploitation of man by another is not preventable. Therefore capital power overwhelms everything else, including central government. The explanation for this is tied to the influential role of corporate power [i.e. big companies or multi-nationals] in national legislative processes and the making of laws.

This is clearly demonstrated by the actions of the current American President, Donald Trump, who is using the power of the presidency in such a way that market efficiency is being hindered by laws which are written in favour of the financially powerful. This can result in a situation where economic growth may increase in a country but the distribution of its goods and services may end up being extremely unfair.

That is, once economic growth is created, there are no economic theories that can be applied to ensure equitable distribution of goods and services. Some people get a larger share than others. Economists tend to leave the job of distribution to others like sociologists, Marxists, politicians etc. Whether capitalism (the free enterprise system we discuss in this book) is better than communism for human beings is outside the scope of this book.

As an example, Sweden follows good economics by adopting the correct economic principles to produce economic growth. But after the wealth has been created, then it is left to the Swedish people to *decide on* a distribution system of its goods and services that benefits all. They tweak it, whereby those who earn more pay progressively higher taxes, relieving those who earn less or nothing. That's why in Sweden the gap between rich and poor is not so visible – it's a welfare state. Yes, this is a case where 8-10 million people can easily agree on something. But can you imagine the chaos in a country of 500 million people? But this book does not enter into a discussion of the merits of a '*socialist state*'. Suffice it to say that, while countries may differ in their political systems, economic theories controlling their decisions and policies remain the same whatever politics they practise.

Have you ever wondered, for instance, why in the USA conservative Republicans always face off liberal Social Democrats? Because there is a difference between know-how, knowledge and social responsibility. That said, we wish to reiterate that this book is totally impartial on political matters. Our only concern is to try and explain how basic economic theories work.

An art teacher may specialize only in '*how to make or do a photo-montage*', but would be unfamiliar with the '*expertise*' needed to judge the '*themes*' that go into the photo-montage materials. Likewise, our aim is not to demystify the politics behind economic results but simply to examine the logic of economic decision-making and its predictable results.

Question 1

(a) Define what economics is all about and state some main theories behind it.

MODEL ANSWER:

Economics is the study of the behavior of human beings in producing, distributing, and consuming material goods and services in a world of scarce resources. Thus, scarcity is the key component in economics studies, because, barring the group of people labeled billionaires, you can never get everything you want at any given point in time. Nevertheless, you are free to strive to acquire or obtain as much as is possible for yourself.

Since people have to *choose*, economic studies focus on how people choose or allocate scarce resources that can be used in alternative ways. Making such choices among equally attractive and beneficial alternatives is perhaps one of the reasons why some people label economics a '*dismal science*'. To facilitate understanding of economic behavior, many economists like to narrow down the theories behind or those affecting economic decisions.

A sample of important theories behind the laws of economics include:

- *The Law of Self-Interest* – that, given a choice, you, as consumer or investor, will always do what is best for yourself. In other words, you will pursue some line of action which will provide you with a material benefit, irrespective of other people's choices.

- *The Law of Demand* – the more there is of a commodity or service, the less people will be willing to pay for it. Conversely, the less of it, the more people will be willing to pay for it. For example, the more workers you have available, the lower would be the wages offered.

- *The Law of Supply* – the more people are willing to pay for something, the more of it other people are going to try to produce. The less people are willing to pay for something, the less of it other people will produce. For example if more cut flowers are demanded in Europe, the greater will be the supply from Africa or other cut flower producers.

- *The Law of Elasticity* – If you are flexible, you pay less, and if you are inflexible, you pay more. Those who only prefer expensive brand names will be prepared to pay more for such items. For example, those who prefer to have the latest cellular phones, such as iPhones, must be prepared to pay more for them. Another example: generic drugs such as HIV/Aids ARVs are cheaper or cost far less than the original brand names.

- *The Law of Economic Reality* – no matter the situation, some combination of these laws will apply. These laws apply in people's everyday lives. Each of us is, as some people put it, *Homo-Economicus.*

Question 2

(a) Define opportunity cost and explain the importance of this concept in economics.

MODEL ANSWER:

The *opportunity cost* of a good is its real cost in terms of alternatives forgone. The purchase of any item involves the sacrifice of other goods. For example, if I buy a car for $12,000 we could say that the cost of the car is the $12,000 that I pay. However, a more revealing way of looking at this transaction is to consider what other goods I could have purchased with the $12,000. Let us say that I could have bought a plot of land. The plot of land is the opportunity cost of buying the car.

The concept of opportunity cost illustrates the Law of Increasing Cost. The more units of a commodity we consume, the greater the sacrifice of self-denial we make for alternative commodities.

This concept of opportunity cost is very useful in economics. It emphasizes two related problems that are central to the study of economics – namely *scarcity* and *choice.* Because resources are scarce, an increase in the consumption of one commodity can only be achieved at the expense of the consumption of other goods. Thus, any type of expenditure involves sacrifice and choice.

The concept of opportunity cost can be used in analyzing individual decisions as well as national choices. Because the consumer has limited resources he has to consider the various alternatives available to him before making any expenditure. Similarly, at the national level, an increase in defense or any other government expenditure can only be achieved at the expense of the provision of other services such as education or health. These considerations obviously have major implications for economic policy at the national level.

The concept of opportunity cost is therefore useful for analyzing national investment decisions over time. In order for the nation to achieve higher rates of economic growth in the future, present consumption has to be wisely controlled or sacrificed altogether. Thus, it is necessary for the nation to invest in capital goods and education. Such investments do not generate an immediate return in terms of goods and services for current consumption and therefore entail opportunity costs in terms of the sacrifice of present consumption.

Question 2

(b) How are the concepts of scarcity, choice and opportunity cost related to the production possibility frontier?

MODEL ANSWER:

The production possibility frontier shows which *alternative combinations of goods* can just be obtained if all the available productive resources of a country are used. This is illustrated in Figure 1.1. Because economic resources are limited in supply, some combinations of goods are beyond the capacity of the economy to produce and are thus unattainable. Such points lie on the right of the curve in the diagram. Points inside the curve can be obtained without using up all the available economic resources (underutilization), while points on the curve can be achieved if the nation's resources are being utilized fully.

The scarcity of economic resources is reflected in the fact that combinations of the two goods that lie outside the production possibility frontier are unobtainable. Choice is reflected in the need for society to select among the various combinations of goods or services that lie on or within the curve. Finally, the concept of opportunity cost is implied by the downward slope of the curve **(Figure 1.1)**

Figure 1.1.

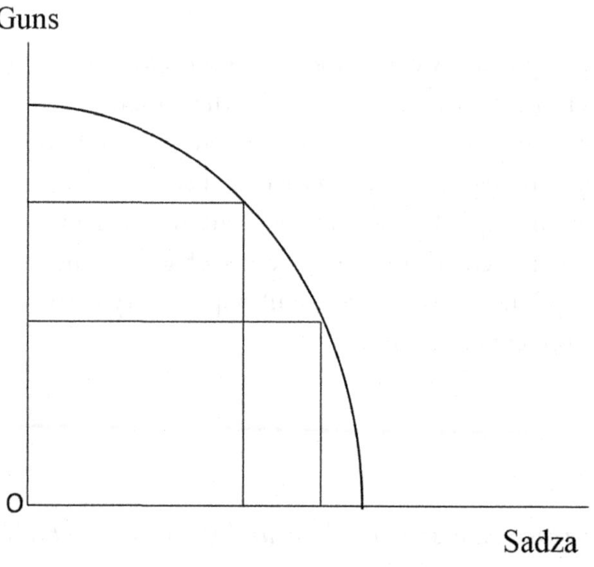

2 Population and Methods of Allocating Resources

Question 1

(a) What factors might cause the population of a country to change?

MODEL ANSWER:
Changes in population may arise in the following ways:

- Natural increase, that is, the excess of births over deaths. This is in turn influenced by the average size of the family and the number of marriages and the availability of medical facilities.
- Changes in immigration and emigration or, more specifically, if the number of people immigrating to the country exceeds the number of people emigrating from the country then, other things being equal, the country's population will increase.

Question 1

(b) Discuss the economic effects of population changes. Illustrate your answer with reference to Zimbabwe and/or Zambia.

MODEL ANSWER:
The economic effects of population changes have to be discussed in relation to the *optimum size* of the population. The optimum population of a country is defined as that size of the population which in conjunction with the country's resources will give rise to maximum output per head.

When the country's population is below the optimum it is desirable to increase the rate of the population growth because this will result in greater utilization of the available resources. Conversely, when the country's population is above the optimum size then it is desirable to reduce the rate of population growth.

Zimbabwe and Zambia's population annual growth rates are similar at 2.3% and 3.0% respectfully.

Another matter to take into consideration is the impact of population size on the supply of labour. An increasing population makes available a greater supply of labour. However, in the context of Zimbabwe or Zambia, this is not a strong argument due to the large number of unemployed people in both countries.

An increasing population may stretch the nation's resources due to the need to provide various forms of social capital such as schools, hospitals and bridges. For example, in Zimbabwe approximately 27% of the national budget goes towards financing education. [Currently 4.7% of GDP in Zimbabwe and 2.0% in Zambia is spent on education].

The economic effects of a population increase also depend on the causes of the increase in population. For example, if it is due to an increase in the birth rate this stimulates demand for baby foods, napkins and so forth. Increased demand for these products in turn stimulates output in industries that are involved in the provision of those items.

On the other hand, if the increase in population is due to the fact that people are living longer this may stretch the nation's resources due to the need to provide various social facilities and services for the elderly. As the demand for social facilities and social services increases, production of the same items will increase.

As far as Zimbabwe or Zambia is concerned, there would seem to be a strong case for reducing the rate of population growth. Zimbabwe's population is currently in excess of 16.5 million and in the case of Zambia it is 16.6 million. The annual rate of population growth in these countries is estimated at 2.5-4% per annum, which is one of the highest rates in Africa. The annual expansion of population is in excess of the rate of growth of GNP while the level of unemployment is high, particularly in rural areas.

Question 2

(a) What are the major features of a free market economy?

MODEL ANSWER:

Under this type of economic system, all major decisions regarding production and distribution of resources are left to the private sector. In relation to the central problems of economics, the problem of what to produce is solved via the medium of the *market* whereby consumers make their wishes felt in the market place. Goods that are not wanted by consumers will suffer a fall in price and producers will cut their production. On the other hand, goods that are high in demand will experience a rise in price so that producers will make more of those goods available. Thus, *price changes* act as a signal to producers as to which goods are in high demand and which ones are in low demand. In such an economic system the *price system* plays a very central role; it indicates the wishes of consumers and, in response, producers provide those goods that the consumers want. In this system, *competition* is the unspoken and unwritten law that (in theory at least) keeps all businesses honest. If the quality of company's product drops without a corresponding adjustment in price – consumers will seek that product from other companies (businesses) who provide a better quality product. When this happens, economists say that company/firm loses its competitive edge.

In a free market the price system also determines the level of production to be adopted. Manufacturers are guided by marginal costs/revenues, where "marginal" refers to how much cost/revenue will be gained or lost by adding or subtracting one unit of whatever is being produced. The cut-off point for production occurs when marginal cost equals marginal revenue.

Inputs into the production process that are in high demand will fetch a high price on the market while those that are in low demand will fetch a low price. Similarly, the distribution of economic resources will take place via the medium of the market without any government interference.

It is the tangible effects of this market efficiency which led Prof. John Galbraith to describe Western countries as "affluent societies". When the marketing system fails to function as it should, it is referred to as 'market failure'.

Question 2

(b) Discuss the advantages and disadvantages of this type of economic system.

MODEL ANSWER:

Two main advantages of the *free market* system may be cited:

* It produces goods and services that consumers actually demand and not, as in a centrally planned economy, where the goods produced are the outcome of some bureaucratic process and not the result of market forces.

* The quality of products is likely to be higher and the range of products wider in such an economy than would most likely be the case in a centrally planned economy.

Firms have an *incentive* to adopt the *most efficient methods* of production because this is one way in which they can stay ahead of competitors.

In theory, a free market system would lead to an efficient allocation of economic resources. This conclusion is based on the assumption that markets are perfectly competitive. In reality however, there are many factors which prevent free markets from operating in the theoretical fashion outlined above – the most important of which are as follows:

* A free market system does not eliminate ignorance among buyers and sellers. The flow of information in the real world is imperfect and economic agents will remain ignorant not only about what is happening in other markets at present, but also what will happen in future. For instance, consumers may not know where to find the products that they want to purchase. Or, producers may refuse to reveal their true intentions for strategic reasons or they may not know where to find the type of employees that they are looking for. For this reason, a free market system will not necessarily lead to an efficient allocation of resources.

* Because richer people have more spending power, they obviously exert a greater influence on the market than poorer people. Thus, a free market system may result in overproduction of those goods which the rich want (such as cars, TVs, stereos, cell phones, and computers) at the expense of basic necessities for the poor.

* The distribution of income generated by the free market system will tend to be unequal because people differ in their natural abilities and physical attributes and therefore, in their potential to earn income.

* In the product market, the operation of the free market mechanism may be subject to imperfections due to the existence of monopolies that restrict output and charge prices that are higher than those that would prevail in a genuinely free market. Firms may get together and make agreements to fix prices so as to eliminate competitors. New firms may be prevented from entering an industry by agreements which favour existing firms.

* In the labour market, certain professions can restrict the entry of new recruits by insisting on high admission standards or long apprenticeship periods. The supply of doctors and lawyers is a good example. Also, trade unions may negotiate contracts with management that make it difficult for employers to dismiss workers. Labour and other factors of production may be immobile for many other reasons. For example, workers may be ignorant about job opportunities in other regions of the country or they may not possess the training needed to undertake certain tasks.

- * Note that our analysis of free market transactions assumed that there are no third-party effects or externalities. Externalities arise if some of the benefits associated with production spill over to third parties who are not directly involved in the production or consumption process. Externalities can be harmful (for example, pollution) or beneficial (for example, a private project in an area with high unemployment creates jobs). When externalities are present, a free market system will under-allocate resources to the production of that commodity or service.

- * A free market system cannot restrict or control the widespread benefits of public goods because those who refuse to pay cannot be stopped from consuming them. *Public goods* are those that cannot be provided to one individual without simultaneously making them available to other citizens (for example, defense, law and order, water supply and sewage treatment).

- * Historically market type economies have generated high levels of unemployment. In a centrally planned economy, the government can influence the level of employment directly through the planning process.

Question 3

(a) What are the major features of a Centrally Planned Economy?

MODEL ANSWER:

In a centrally planned (or command or communist) economy all the means of production and distribution are controlled by the state. All economic decisions are made by a powerful central planning authority or committees whose job is to specify production targets or quotas for the different firms (or industries) in the economy and allocate resources to these firms (or industries) to enable them to achieve the productions goals set for them. In addition, workers may be assigned to certain occupations or to certain geographical areas. Surplus where it occurs is destroyed to create artificial scarcity or shortages. The following are among the main advantages of this type of economic system:

* The central planning authority has the ability to control and co-ordinate economic activity in the economy. In this way, the authority can ensure that the nation's social and economic objectives are achieved. By contrast, in a free market economy such decisions are left to private individuals and there is no guarantee that individual actions will be in line with the nation's social and economic objectives.

* In a market economy, consumer preferences are supposed to signal to producers the range of goods that should be produced. However, such preferences may merely reflect the decisions of those who have the income and wealth to make their influence felt on the market. In contrast, a centrally planned economy has the ability to assess the preferences of society at large regardless of income or social status.

* In a centrally planned economy, the planners can explicitly consider future generations in current decisions. A good example of that is the Chinese economy. By contrast, in a market economy, decisions are the outcome of the market mechanism and as such do not explicitly take into account future generations.

* A centrally planned economy can take into account mechanisms particularly as regards externalities, monopolies, unequal distribution of income and wealth and so forth which affect consumption patterns.

Question 3

(b) Outline the major disadvantages of this type of economic system.

MODEL ANSWER:
On the other hand a centrally planned economy suffers from a number of defects among which the following should be noted:

* There is always a danger that the central planning authority may abuse its powers. The excessive concentration of power in a few individuals can be used to restrict individual rights and freedom.

* Decisions made by the central planning authority are far reaching. If mistakes are made, they will be more damaging that in a market economy where the process of decision-making is left to individuals.

* The quality of products and the range of goods available is usually inferior to that in a market economy because firms in a centrally planned economy are not under the same competitive pressures as those in a free market economy.

* In a centrally planned economy, many officials are needed to estimate consumer needs and the inputs needed in the process of production. This can give rise to excessive bureaucracy. In a market economy such officials are not needed since consumer wants are established automatically through the free operation of the price system.

* A centrally planned economy may reduce incentives to work. If workers are moved to jobs that they do not enjoy performing, morale will be low and efficiency may decline as a result.

3 Determination of Price in a Free Market and the Consumer Theory

Question 1

(a) Can you briefly describe consumer demand

MODEL ANSWER:

In an economy where various kinds of goods and services are produced, a consumer demands or buys a bundle of those goods and services for which he/she is *willing and able to pay*. These goods and services are those from which the consumer can derive some utility or satisfaction of sorts.

- Being able to pay for goods and services means that the specific prices for those goods and services are affordable. Thus, the quantity demanded depends, first and foremost on the good's price. Therefore to determine the price, and hence quantity, economists usually hold all other factors constant (so called ceteris paribus).

- In this ceteris-paribus case, other factors held constant include: *income, preferences*, and the *price* of other goods and services. When for example you have more income, the quantity and assortment of goods and services you demand increases. With less income, you tend to consume less and generally tend to go for cheaper goods and services.

- Likewise, the quantity demanded is also affected by tastes and preferences. Those who love ice cream in summer will not suddenly stop buying it in the next summer season even if the price goes up. And those who hate it, will not start buying it even if the price went down. Thus, some people have a higher demand or more preference for certain goods and services than others.

- And when prices on other goods and services fall or increase, this may affect the demand of other similar goods. A good example: if the price of beef goes up, consumers may switch to buying more chicken. Or if the average price of a concert becomes too expensive, for leisure people may instead switch to movies.

Note that - to carefully study the demand curve, only the price is shown on the *analytical graphs*, holding everything else constant. Under these conditions – prices have an *inverse relationship* with the quantity demanded. That is, the higher the price, the less quantity is demanded, and vice versa. See **Figure 3.1**

Figure 3.1

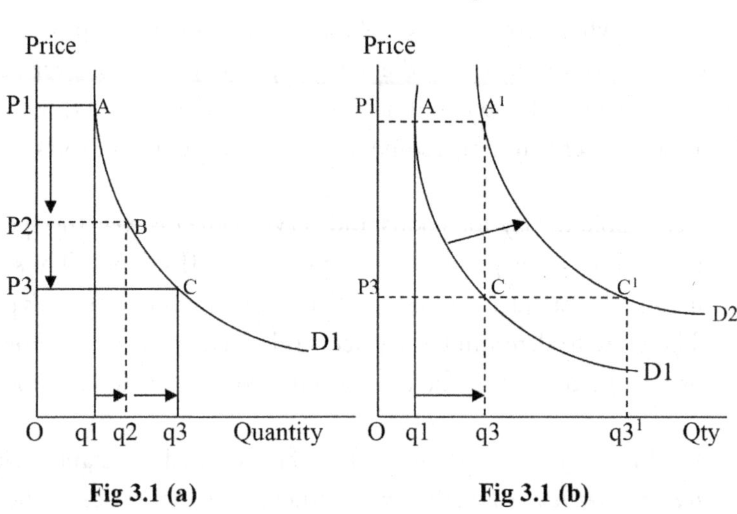

Fig 3.1 (a) **Fig 3.1 (b)**

In **Figure 3.1(a)**: when the price falls, the greater the quantity of tomatoes purchased. Fig3.1 (b): represents an increase in demand for tomatoes. The demand curve *shifts right* (D1 to D2) but due to *non-price factors*. But at the same price of P1, point A[1] yields greater quantity than at point A.

In **Figure (a),** the demand-curve is *drawn sloping* **up** because as prices fall, consumers buy more. For example, when the price of tomatoes drop from say (P1) to (P2), the quantity of tomatoes bought rises from q1 to q2 – a *shift along* the demand-curve from point A to B. A shift from (P2) to (P3), more tomatoes q2 to q3 are bought. An increase or decrease *in price* moves you along the demand-curve.

But a complete shift of the demand-curve to the right is caused by *non-price factors* such as: changes in income, tastes or preferences. For example, a nutritional study which shows that consumption of vegetables such as tomatoes (vitamins source) and beans (protein source) improves nutrition and health of people might spark an *increase* in the consumption of vegetables and beans. In this case, the demand-curve then moves *entirely* to the right. This is illustrated in **Figure (b).** Conversely, if the demand for a product *decreases*, the demand-curve shifts *entirely* to the left.

In **Figure 3.1(b)**, note that: point A on demand-curve D1 and A^1 on demand-curve D2 share the same price of (P1). Since at point A^1 you are consuming more tomatoes/beans than before, this shows that the change is due to something else other than price.

Question 1

(b) *With the aid of diagrams and suitable examples illustrate the economic effects of price controls.*

MODEL ANSWER:

Price controls can be subdivided into two main categories namely *maximum price controls* and *minimum price controls.* These are discussed in more detail below.

Price control tends to interfere with firms'/consumers' decisions. The firms' aim to maximize their profits coupled with the desires of consumers helps to guide their decisions regarding production and the allocation of resources. When there are no price controls, the *equilibrium* position or *optimal level* (the best) is achieved when consumers get their maximum satisfactions from a combination of goods and services and sellers maximize their profits by producing goods and services at different and appropriate levels of output.

The essential nature or purpose of price control, such as *price ceiling,* is that the government intervenes to ensure that the price stays below the market equilibrium Pm. [i.e., P1 sets a price ceiling]. But because the quantity supplied Qs is less than the quantity demanded Qd, there is a shortage (Qd – Qs)...see **Figure 3.2** below.

(i) Maximum price legislation

In certain cases the government may feel that the market price of certain commodities is *too high*. It may then set a lower price for these commodities than that which would be established in a free market. In Zimbabwe, a number of commodities have been subjected to price controls of this nature since independence in 1980. Zambia used price controls prior to 1991 multiparty politics. The basic objective of the price control system is to set prices at a level which the poorer people can afford. Such controls are sometimes referred to as *price ceilings* because government orders prevent the prices of specific goods from rising above a certain level.

Figure 3.2

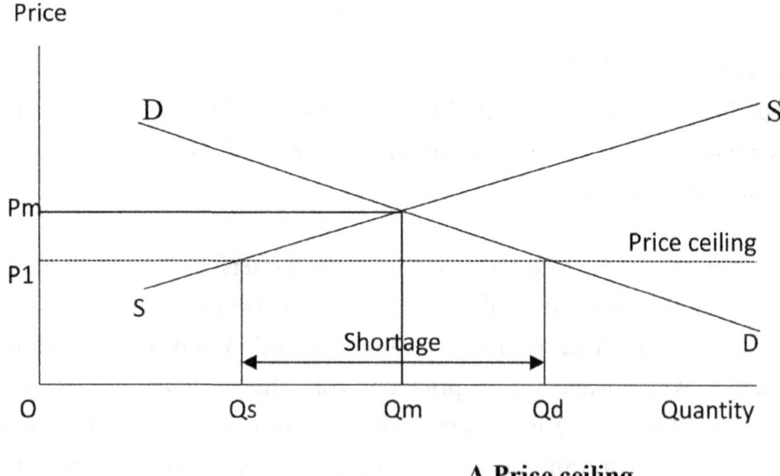

A Price ceiling

The impact of ***price ceilings*** is illustrated in **Figure 3.1**. The government sets a maximum price P1 when the free market price would be Pm. At this price, quantity demanded is Q1 (Q_D) and the quantity supplied Q2 (Q_S). Thus, with price controls, there is a shortage of the commodity, equal to ($Q_D - Q_S$). In a free market, such shortages would result in upward pressure on the price level. In this case, however, the price cannot increase beyond the limit set by the government P1 (the ceiling). Thus, in an environment of price controls, the allocative function of the free market is destroyed. (Note, however, that if the price ceiling is set above the free market price, Pm, it has no effect.)

Rent control policies present good examples of how price ceilings work. These are practiced in a number of countries, including Zambia and Zimbabwe. Rent controls have a number of effects. For one thing, landlords may refuse to make essential repairs to property because their incomes are controlled, thereby reducing quality, or they may ask potential tenants for a non-refundable deposit as a condition for obtaining accommodation. Rent controls tend to cause shortages, resulting in queues or long waiting lines. For commodities which are necessities, like sugar, shortages may encourage black market activities.

(ii) Minimum price legislation

In some cases the government may feel that the market price is *too low*, e.g. price of milk per liter. If so, it may set a minimum price at which the commodity should be sold. Such price controls are known as *price floors,* because the price is not allowed to fall below a certain level. The effect of setting a minimum price is illustrated in **Figure 3.3**. The free market price is given by P0. The government feels that this is too low and sets a price floor at P1. At this price, the quantity of the commodity demanded is Q1 and the quantity supplied is Q2. Thus, there is a *surplus* of the commodity equal to Q2-Q1. To deal with the problem of surpluses the government may restrict the supply of the commodity to Q2 or it may store the excess supply and release the stocks when demand increases.

Figure 3.3

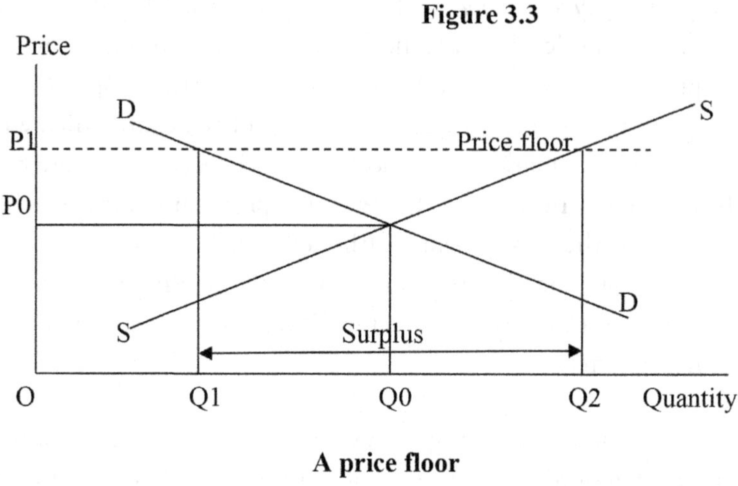

A price floor

(i) One good example of the minimum price model is displayed by the setting of *producer prices* on crops such as maize (corn) above the market level. To encourage farmers or as a way of raising their incomes, the government may decide to set a minimum selling price for a bag of maize. For milk, if producers are believed to be making too little money, government sets a minimum price of say eighty cents (80c) – P1 from PO, sixty cents (60c) per liter. **[see Figure 3.3 again].**

Once set, the government prevents the price from falling below this price floor. To adjust or clear the market, the government usually steps in and buys all excess supply. Hence, the term *price supports.* In USA, these price supports are often used to help dairy farmers or grain producers. The disadvantage of these price supports is that they may result in huge surpluses which cannot be sold at market prices. This generates losses and wastage of taxpayers' resources.

As illustrated in a *floor price,* the quantity demanded (Q1) is against the quantity supplied (Q2). This causes a surplus of (qS – qD). The question arises as to what to do with such surpluses. Also in essence consumers end up paying a higher price but receive less output though there are surpluses. A number of ways to eliminate these surpluses have been tried in countries like United States of America – among them: donating these surpluses as food to poor countries, or converting surpluses to powder or cheese in case of milk, or simply destroying or burning surpluses such as in the case of grains.

In USA and EU countries, sometimes the excess supply, which results from a policy of agricultural *subsidies,* is solved by paying farmers not to produce the oversupplied items. One wonders why this tool is discouraged or not used in Less Developed African Countries (LDAC) as an incentive to produce much-needed foodstuffs.

(ii) Another example of price floors can be observed with *minimum wage legislation.*

Many governments set a minimum wage for workers in order to reduce the level of poverty, to the extent that the minimum wage is higher than the equilibrium wage. This creates a surplus of workers on the labour market. Two related factors help to create a surplus:

- with higher wages more people will want to work.
- but when the level of wages is high employers will be inclined to reduce the number of workers they employ so as to cut their costs of production (**Figure 3.4**).

To begin with, assume that the expected price is P0 and the planned level of output Q0. Let Dx and De represent two alternative demand curves. The curves have been drawn in such a way that Dx is *inelastic* while De is *elastic.* Unplanned variations in supply will cause prices to fluctuate between Q1 and Q2. When demand is inelastic (Dx) prices will show large fluctuations. However, when demand is elastic (De) price fluctuations will be much smaller.

Figure 3.4

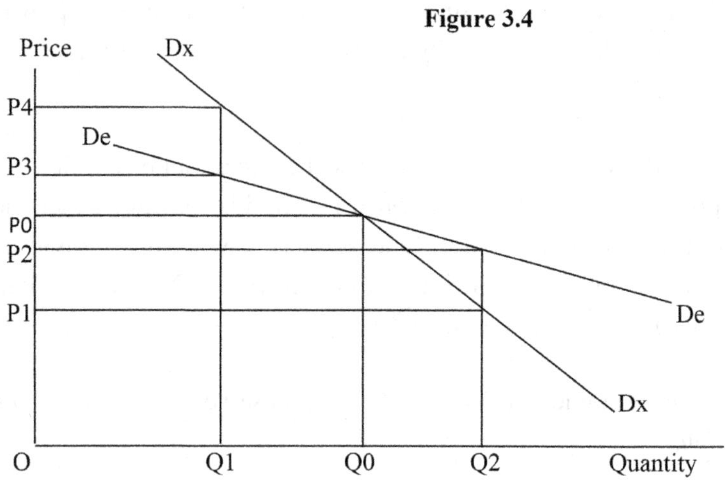

Politicians in charge of government prefer policies that will produce good results, although in some cases that doesn't happen. This is especially so when legislation is initiated for non-economic reasons but purely political ones. Looking at it carefully, you'll discover that *minimum wage laws* actually raise unemployment. That is, the unemployment situation is aggravated instead. Just as sometimes rent control laws fail to control rent.

Such outcomes are surprising to many people. Many of the unintended consequences of these policies and programs can be avoided if these processes are analyzed in terms of the incentives and constraints they can potentially create, instead of only looking at the desirability of the goals or objectives themselves. That is, the chain of events policies can set in motion may be unforeseen and unintended.

Another example: repairing of potholes may be neglected because that work has less of an immediate visible effect in relation to the government's goals, incentives or constraints. Hence, considerations in terms of wear and tear are not prioritized. This is one explanation as to why potholes are neglected.

What economic analysis (using cost-benefit analysis) does in such a situation is to systematically examine the consequences of various economic actions and policies, then choose one (or lets the authorities choose one) that is most beneficial. The choice is the one where the utilization and use of limited resources (e.g. labour or human capital) is fully utilized. In other words, one must consider how good the results are given the real situation. Thus, the consequences can be used to determine how well-off or worse-off a country becomes after a policy action.

When passing minimum wage legislation, for example, it is important for us to look at them critically instead of letting them pass without serious thought. So, if pay was to be based on productivity then workers would tend to seek higher paying jobs. In such a situation, labour value tends to approach that of capital. Therefore when you hear about minimum-wage riots or protests, that should not surprise anyone.

Labour laws such as minimum-wage laws or belonging to labour unions are vehicles which act as moderators between employers and employees in a free market economy and should not be viewed as a model to exploit workers. While employers, who are the investors of capital and machinery, have a right to earn a return, the amount of those profits should not be exploitative, i.e. not at the expense of workers (labour). A clearer understanding of this challenge can be obtained by comparing the labour situation in Zimbabwe, Zambia and South Africa.

Discussing the labour situation of Zimbabwe and Zambia, with a focus on the minimum-wage, and including neighboring countries like South Africa in that discussion, can be extremely sensitive. Less than twenty years ago South Africa was under the *Apartheid* system where a lot of 'black labour' (or human capital) was not free to negotiate with employers or 'unfree' in the sense that the *pay* was very poor, hence, the specifics of that peculiar labour situation do not easily lend themselves to classical analysis. That is because a lot of South Africa's labour was either compulsory or involuntary (in a word, forced). And in some extreme cases, there was no financial compensation at all or workers were used as 'slave labour'. Therefore, the transition from a 'no-pay' for labour situation to a minimum-wage one may be hard to fully comprehend.

We also need to consider factors on the demand side that affect prices. For many primary products variations in foreign demand are an important source of price fluctuations. Note that: these shifts may occur in response to cyclical changes in incomes in importing countries (if the commodity in question is exported), or in response to changes in the prices of substitutes, or due to other factors. The effects of these shifts in price and output will depend on the elasticity of supply of the commodity in question. In general, primary products tend to be *inelastic in supply* because the factors of production used in producing them (such as land) tend to be specific to that use (that is, they cannot be easily transferred to alternative uses). Therefore, given an inelastic supply, variations in supply will therefore have a large impact on demand.

On the other hand, for goods that are *elastic in supply* (such as industrial products) demand shifts will have a large impact on output but little effect on price. These two effects are illustrated in **Figure 3.5** and **Figure 3.6**, whereas **Figure 3.5** shows an *inelastic supply and* **Figure 3.6** an *elastic supply curve.* A perfectly inelastic supply curve is vertical – i.e., price has no effect on quantity supplied at all. And a perfectly *elastic* supply is *horizontal* – i.e., beyond a certain price, (above horizontal line) you supply nothing.

These two diagrams show that a shift in demand from D1 – D2 (**Figure 3.5**) and D1-D0 (**Figure 3.6**) will result in a much larger price change when supply is inelastic than when it is elastic. For all these reasons, the prices of primary products are often subject to wide fluctuations.

Figure 3.5 **Figure 3.6**

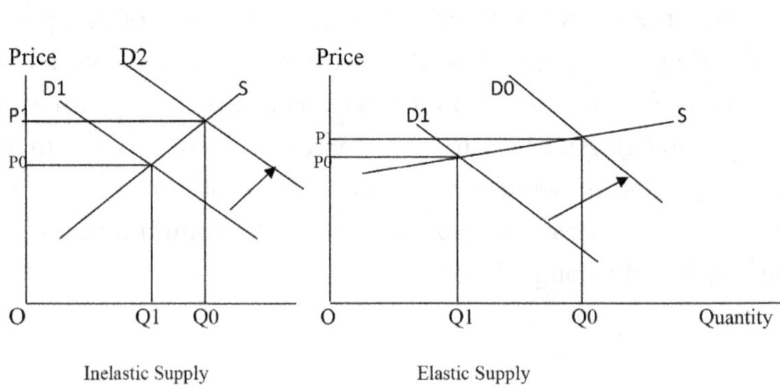

Question 2

(a) Briefly discuss the elasticity of supply.

MODEL ANSWER:

Elasticity of Supply **(Es)** measures the *responsiveness of the quantity supplied* by sellers to a rise or fall in price. This is expressed as: -

$$Es = \frac{\Delta Qs \text{ \% change in quantity supplied}}{\Delta Ps \text{ \% change in price}}$$

Es = Is coefficient of supply elasticity

Note: When Es = 0.5 (or 5/10), that implies a 10% change in price would lead to a 5% rise in output (supply).

When supply coefficient is less than one, it means that supply is inelastic; equal to one, it is unitary supply; and more than one, it means supply is elastic. **Figure 3.7 and Figure 3.8** drawn without demand below illustrate *inelastic* supply and *elastic* supply respectively as price changes.

Figure 3.7 **Figure 3.8**

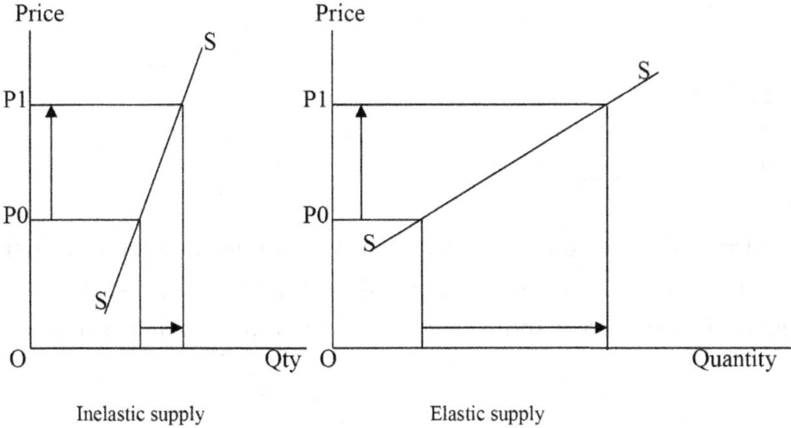

Inelastic supply

Elastic supply

Figure 3.7 illustrates that quantity supplied changes much ***less than*** the change in price (i.e., supply is inelastic). And **Figure 3.8** illustrates that quantity supplied changes ***more than*** the changes in price (i.e., supply is elastic). In a similar fashion, both *inelastic* and *elastic* demand could be illustrated as price changes.

Question 2

(b) Discuss factors affecting elasticity of supply.

MODEL ANSWER:

There are three main factors affecting supply elasticity: (i) *Time*: the longer the time the seller has to adjust or increase production, the more elastic the supply is. In the short run, the supply of vegetables for example, may be inelastic but becomes elastic in the longer term when supply becomes plentiful. (ii) *Cost considerations:* Increase in production may be costly for certain industries; costly inputs may hinder quick production especially in the short term. For example, in the short term, demand for a product may be up, but suppliers may be unable to meet the supply needs due to limitations in, say, availability of raw materials. (iii) *Ease of storage*: when a price drops, depending on the type of product, the seller can choose to sell it at that new low price or store it as an inventory and sell it later when the price improves. These products which can easily be stored tend to have a greater elasticity of supply.

Question 2

(c) Briefly discuss elasticity of demand.

To understand the actions/decisions taken by consumers and suppliers in the marketplace, economists use concepts like *elasticity*, or the responsiveness of quantities demanded and supplied in relation to the changes in price.

Where: *price elasticity of demand* (**Ed**) is a formula or explanation to measure the actual change in quantity demanded for a product or service whose price has changed. It is expressed as: -

Ed = ΔQd or Coefficient of demand elasticity

$$Ed = \frac{\Delta Qd \quad \text{\% change in quantity demanded}}{\Delta Pd \quad \text{\% change in price}}$$

Note: If Ed = 0.5 (or 5/10), it implies that a 10% decrease in price leads to 5% increase in demand.

That is, since the change in price affects people's decisions, the effect is felt in the quantity demanded. If price elasticity of demand (Ed) is between one and zero, the coefficient is *inelastic*. This means that a percentage change in price causes only a smaller percentage change in quantity demanded. When Ed is greater than one, it means demand is elastic. And when Ed is equal to one, it is unitary coefficient – i.e., a percentage change in price results in an equal percentage change in quantity demanded. Diagrams **Figure 3.9 and Figure 3.10** below illustrate inelastic demand and elastic demand respectively.

Figure 3.9 **Figure 3.10**

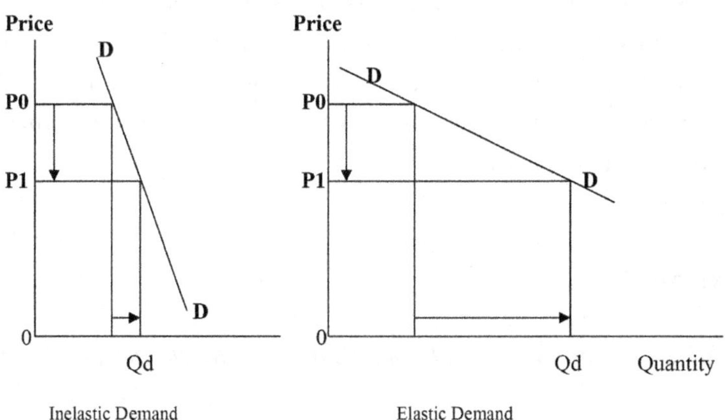

Inelastic Demand Elastic Demand

A perfectly *inelastic* demand curve is *vertical* – i.e., price has no effect on demand. For example, price is not important on life-saving drugs such as ARVs to HIV/Aids patients. A small change in price has a large change in quantity demanded.

A perfectly *elastic* demand is *horizontal* – i.e., you either buy everything or nothing. An example is two i-Phone brands which provide exactly the same features.

Question 2

(d) Discuss factors affecting demand elasticity.

MODEL ANSWER:

There are four main factors affecting demand elasticity: (i) *Availability of substitutes*: Single brand products like chocolate candy tend to be elastic because there are no close substitutes. That is, consumers cannot easily switch. (ii) *Necessities or essential goods* tend to be more inelastic than *luxury* items. The price change on say bread does affect the quantities demanded significantly as compared to cigarettes. (iii) *Income*: If the fraction of one's income spent on an item is large, such as expenditure on capital items like furniture, or if the prices of those goods rise steeply, then people just do without them or postpone the purchase until they can afford it. This change affected by affordability is said to be price elastic. (iv) *Time*: The amount of time available to look for goods also has an effect on demand. If over time consumers can find substitutes, the demand tends to be elastic. In the short run, when people don't have information on the availability of alternatives or are not even aware of substitutes, then the demand for these goods can be inelastic.

Question 3

(a) With the aid of a numerical example define price elasticity of demand.

MODEL ANSWER:

As defined by economists, the concept of elasticity of demand measures how well quantity demanded responds to a given change in price. Although the law of price states that the quantity demanded increases as price falls, this is not true of all goods at all times. For instance, for an individual who is heavily addicted to cigarettes, a fall in their price will not, in all probability, lead him to reduce his consumption.

Numerically, the elasticity of demand can be measured using the formula:

$$\frac{\%\text{ change in quantity demanded}}{\%\text{ change in price}}$$

For example, suppose that a 10% reduction in price leads to a 5% increase in quantity demanded, the price elasticity of demand is:

$$\frac{5}{10} = 0.5$$

The value for the price elasticity of demand will lie between zero and infinity and the interpretation of these values is as follows:

**When the value is equal to zero,* this means that change in price will have no effect whatsoever on quantity demanded; you either buy all or nothing. The horizontal demand curve is said to be perfectly elastic. Conversely, a vertical demand-curve is said to be perfectly inelastic when the consumer is prepared to pay any price to obtain the item (i.e., an exact number of Q-units are demanded no matter what the price is).

* *When the value is less than one,* then a change in price will have a less than proportionate effect on quantity demanded. Demand is said to be inelastic.

* *When the value is less than one,* then a change in price will have more than proportionate effect on quantity demanded. Demand is said to be elastic.

* *When the value is equal to one,* then a change in demand will have a proportionate effect on quantity demanded. Demand is said to be unit elastic.

* *A demand curve of infinite elasticity* means that at a certain price, consumers will purchase unlimited quantities of the commodity while at another price, they will purchase none at all.

* *For understanding the functioning of markets.* For example, in the theory of the firm, perfectly competitive firms are assumed to have a perfect elastic demand curve. Because of this, none of the firms can influence the price of the commodity. This assumption has important implications for the behavior of the firm under perfectly competitive conditions.

* *For the analysis of business decisions.* Before changing the price of his product, a businessman needs to consider its elasticity of demand. When demand is elastic it will be profitable for him to reduce his price because total revenue will increase. Conversely, when demand for the product is inelastic a price reduction will lead to a fall in revenue.

* *In international trade,* when analyzing the effects of depreciation or devaluation on the balance of payments. It can be shown that a depreciation or devaluation of the currency will only be successful in correcting the balance of payments when the demand for exports and imports is elastic.

Question 3

(b) What is the importance of this demand elasticity concept in economics?

MODEL ANSWER:

Within the area of government finance, the concept of elasticity of demand is useful when the government is considering whether to impose sales taxes. In order to earn maximum revenue from sales tax, it is essential that there is inelastic demand for the commodities selected. When this is the case, an increase in sales taxes will lead to a less than proportionate fall in quantity demand and total revenue will increase.

Question 4

(a) How does the market determine the equilibrium price?

MODEL ANSWER

The equilibrium price is reached when the demand curve (D) and supply curve (S) come together and *intersect.* Point A in the diagram, (**Figure 3.11**) determines both the equilibrium price **(P*)** and the equilibrium quantity **(Q*).** At point A, consumers who seek the lowest prices possible and sellers who want the highest prices compromise.

At equilibrium price, the desires of buyers and sellers match each other, resulting in the quantity demanded equaling the quantity supplied. In a free market system, this state is maintained by market forces. Whenever the price is *greater than* P*, this situation causes a surplus or oversupply. Adjustments occur by sellers lowering the price to clear the surplus. Price P* is again attained.

Figure 3.11

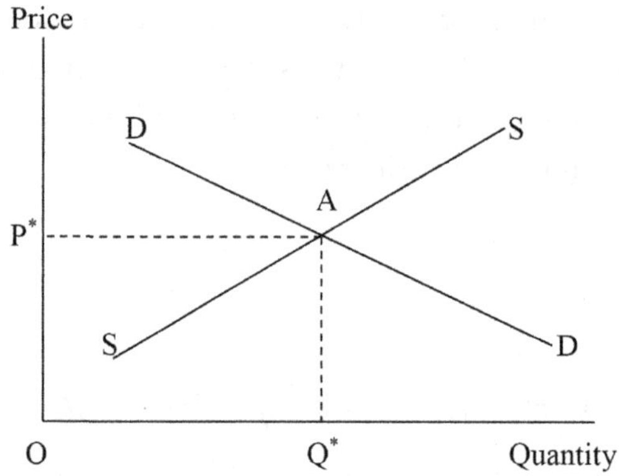

Market Equilibrium Price & Quantity

Conversely, at a price *lower than* P*, fewer goods would be supplied against a higher demand, causing a shortage. Faced with a shortage, buyers bid higher prices which incentivizes the sellers to produce more. Once again P* is restored. Hence in a market, there is always a tendency to move towards the *equilibrium* price P*; where the quantity supplied (Qs) will be equal to the quantity demanded (Qd). Thus, Qs = Qd. Unless there is an external disturbance or intervention, this process towards *equilibrium* position holds. Thus, equilibrium is a point where both consumers and producers are happy.

Question 4

(b) Describe the functions of price in a free market.

MODEL ANSWER:
In a free market, price performs many functions.

It acts as a *rationing device* for scarce economic resources through the interaction of supply and demand without any government intervention.

The supply of economic resources is limited and has to be rationed among the many people who want to access those resources.

To illustrate the rationing function of price, let us suppose that demand and supply are in equilibrium initially and that the price level rises. As a result of the price increase, demand will increase (that is, shift to the right). The higher price makes it more profitable for the producer to supply the product. Thus, supply will increase and equilibrium will be restored at a lower price and higher quantity. The equilibrium price clears the market and leaves no shortages for consumers and no surpluses for producers. The interaction of supply and demand sets a price that clears the market. In the absence of such a mechanism, some form of administrative control would be required to bring supply and demand into equilibrium and deal with the problems of surpluses and shortages.

In **Figure 3.12**, S0-S0 and D0-D0 represent the initial supply and demand curves and P0 and Q0 represent the initial equilibrium price and quantity respectively. An increase in demand from D0-D0 to D1-D1 leads to a rise in price from P0-P1. This makes it more profitable to supply the commodity and producers respond by increasing supply from S0-S0 to S1-S1. The effect is to reduce price to a new equilibrium P2.

Figure 3.12

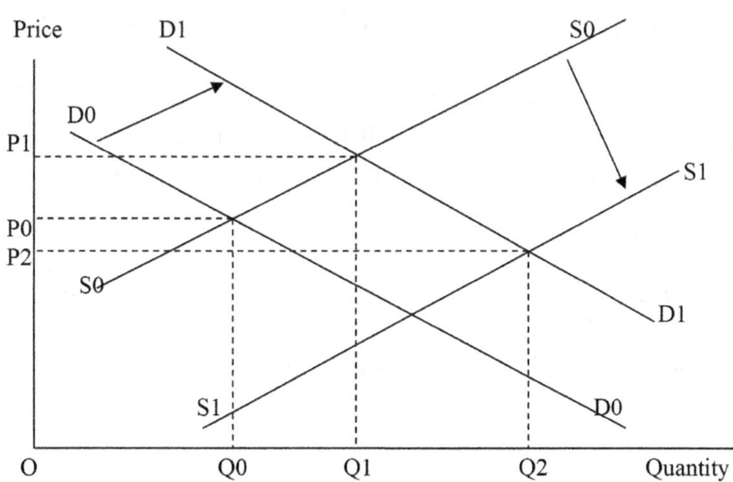

Further, in a free market the price is the *median* through which consumers reveal their preferences for different commodities. Goods for which there is a big demand experience a rise in price and the supply of those goods increases. By the same argument, commodities for which demand is low experience a fall in price and less of them are produced.

Affecting the price of products and levels of profit are changes in consumer taste which result in the expansion of some industries and the contraction of others. These adjustments feed through the market and impact factors of production as expanding industries demand more factors of production.

The price system also provides incentives to use high technology and cost minimizing techniques of production. Improvements in technology, to the extent that they are cost minimizing, give one firm the edge over its rivals and the benefits of lower costs of production which can then be passed on to the consumer in the form of lower prices. Similarly, the economic environment provided by the free market is conducive to the rapid diffusion of technology. Because of the benefits to be gained from lower costs of production rival firms are under pressure to follow the example of the more aggressive, innovative firms.

Finally, the price system affects the way in which income is distributed among the factors of production. For example, a rise in the price of a commodity means that firms are able to pay a higher reward to their factors. Similarly, higher prices result in higher profits for the entrepreneur.

Thus, *given the specific assumptions on which the free market model is based,* the operation of the price system will result in an efficient allocation of resources among all the competing demands in the economy.

Question 5

(a) Can you briefly define consumption choices?

MODEL ANWER:

Making a choice of what to buy is not a straight forward matter. Our purchases are influenced by such factors as the *utility* we get from the goods or services we buy. Economists use the *marginal utility theory of consumer choice,* or simply *utility theory,* to analyze this **problem**.

The "satisfaction", "enjoyment" or "usefulness" one gets by consuming something is described as "**utility**". The mangoes I buy show that I enjoy them. But whatever ***"extra"*** **utility** or *marginal utility* I get by buying another mango helps to determine consumption choices.

Question 5

(b) Define diminishing marginal utility.

MODEL ANSWER:

The word "utility" means the ability to satisfy a want. The hypothesis of a diminishing marginal utility states that *the utility a consumer derives from the consumption of successive units of a commodity or service diminishes as the consumption of that commodity increases, holding constant the consumption of all other goods.*

Question 5

(c) Given two goods X and Y, how does a consumer achieve equilibrium?

MODEL ANSWER: I

To achieve equilibrium, a utility maximizing consumer will adjust his expenditure between commodities in such a way that the utility of the last cent spent on each commodity is equal. The explanation for this is as follows. Suppose the utility of the last cent spent on beer is three times that spent on cigarettes. If so, the consumer's total utility can be increased by switching expenditure as long as one cent of beer yields more utility than a cent spent on cigarettes. The switching will stop only when the utility of a cent spent on beer *just equals* the utility of a cent spent on cigarettes. When this stage is reached, the consumer is said to be *in equilibrium.*

Another way of looking at this problem is as follows. Let the marginal utility of the last unit of good X be represented by MUx and the price of commodity X by Px. Likewise, let the marginal utility of good Y be represented by MUy and the price by Py. Given this information, the condition for the consumer to be in equilibrium is:

$$\frac{MUx}{Px} = \frac{MUy}{Py}$$

This is just another way of saying that the utility of the last cent spent on good X should equal the utility of one cent spent on good Y. If we cross multiply the above we get:

$$\frac{MUx}{MUy} = \frac{Px}{Py}$$

This says that the utility of the last units of X and Y consumed must be proportional to the prices of X and Y.

Question 5

(d) *What happens to consumer equilibrium if the price of one of the commodities falls?*

MODEL ANSWER: II

If the price of good Y falls (with the price of X remaining constant), the *marginal utility* of Y rises relative to X. To restore equilibrium, the marginal utility of Y must be decreased. This can be achieved by purchasing more units of Y. On the other hand, if the price of Y rises, the marginal utility of Y decreases relative to X and the consumer can restore equilibrium by reducing the consumption of Y.

Question 6

(a) Can you restate diminishing marginal utility in a two goods world?

MODEL ANSWER:

Given two products – let say, mangoes versus ice cream, the choice for purchase depends on the *utility* one gets from each good. If one has been buying too many mangoes and fewer ice creams, we say that the utility one gets from consuming one more mango is lower than that obtainable from consuming one more ice cream.

If one wants to balance and thus *maximize the consumption* of the two items, then one must compare the *marginal utilities* of both in relation to each good's price. Limited by a consumer's budget, utility is maximized for both goods (the best combination of consuming the two products) when the *marginal utility* (MU) of each product *divided by its price* is equal to one another. That is, one aims for a combination that yields the largest possible amount of utility.

For goods X (mangoes) and Y (ice cream), this is expressed as:

$$\frac{\text{MUx}}{\text{Price of x}} = \frac{\text{MUy}}{\text{Price of y}}$$

This expression also tells us that, as people consume more, the "*extra satisfaction*" or utility they get *declines*. (See Table 3). In other words, the higher the utility, the higher the price consumers are willing to pay. Diamonds are expensive because their scarcity results in an extremely high level of satisfaction for those who purchase them. In contrast, water, which is essential for life but relatively plentiful in supply, has a lower marginal utility and is therefore cheap. By using utility theory, Adam Smith was able to solve the paradox of why necessities such as water is cheaper when compared to scarce luxury items such as diamonds.

Question 7

(b) What is consumer surplus?

MODEL ANSWER:

The *consumer surplus* measures the difference between the market prices and the maximum price the consumer *would be willing to pay* to obtain a unit of a commodity. A simple example might help to illustrate this concept. Suppose a consumer purchases a bag of maize for $25 but in fact would be prepared to pay as much as $30 for the bag. If so, his consumer surplus for the purchase is $5.

Figure 3.13 illustrates the concept. The consumer surplus is the shaded area under the demand curve above the price line. That shaded area under the demand curve shows the total valuation the consumer places on all units of that commodity. From **Figure 3.13** we can see that the total valuation of Q0 units of the commodity is the entire area under the demand curve up to Q0. The consumer surplus is the area above P0 under the demand curve.

Figure 3.13

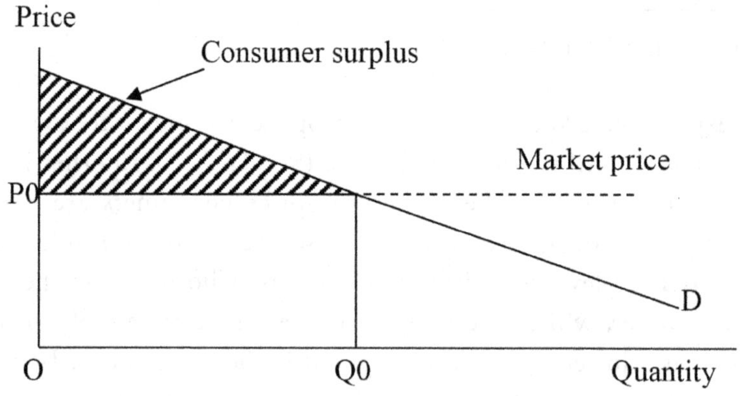

(b) Explain why demand curves slope towards from left to right.

Question 7

(c) Explain why the demand curve slopes downward from left to right.

MODEL ANSWER:

The demand curve slopes downwards from left to right due to the operation of *income* and *substitution effects*. A fall in the price leads to an increase in the individual's ***real income.*** This will be reflected in a higher demand for the consumer product. Conversely, an increase in price leads to a fall in real income. These changes are referred to as the income effects of a price change.

Changes in price also result in substitution effects. If the price of commodity x rises while the prices of other commodities remain constant, the consumer will substitute more of the cheaper commodities for the one that has gone up in price. This is the ***substitution effect*** of the price change.

The combination of income and substitution effects explains the downward slope of the demand curve shown in **Figure 3.14.** At higher prices consumers will purchase less of a commodity while at lower prices they will purchase more of it (at Q1 and Q2 respectively). That is, consumers will buy more of the commodity only if its price falls.

Figure 3.14

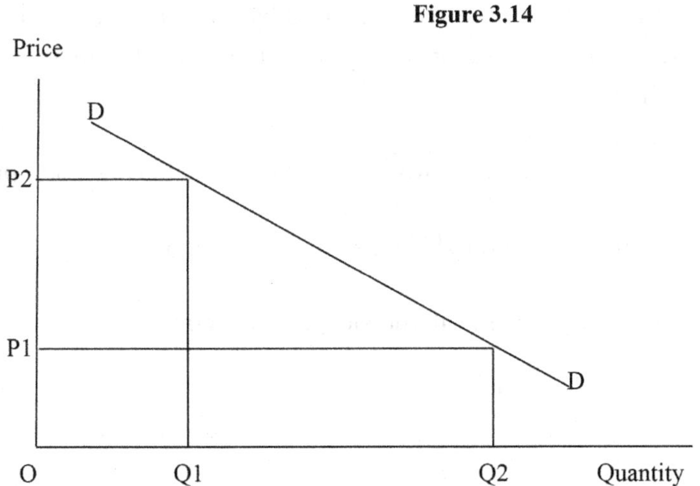

4 Production and Theory of the Firm

Question 1

(a) State what you understand by the law of diminishing returns and explain clearly how it works. Use a diagram to explain your answer.

MODEL ANSWER:

The law of diminishing returns (LDR) states that *as we add successive units of a variable factor to fixed quantities of other factors, there will, beyond a certain point, be a less than proportional increase in total output.* In other words, in any production process, the amount added to output from each additional unit of input decreases as you use more and more of the input. As diminishing returns set in, the production process eventually starts costing more, hence the necessity for the firm to establish a cut-off point for each input's contribution to total output (such as, for instance, limiting the number of workers employed by the firm). To get the most out of each input the firm or society must therefore allocate or reassign inputs optimally.

To demonstrate how this law works we make the following assumptions:

- All units of the variable factor are homogenous
- The state of technical knowledge is constant

- The quantity of other inputs is constant
- The proportions in which the factors of production can be combined must be capable of variation.

Given these assumptions, using one fixed factor (land) and one variable factor (labour) we can show how the law works as illustrated in **Figure 4.1** and **Table 4.1**. From the table, we can see that starting from zero, the effect of increasing the supply of the *variable factor* causes total output to rise but, after a certain point, the marginal and the average production impact of the variable factor start to decline as more units of the variable factor is added to the production process.

Table 4.1

Total Product	Fixed Costs	Variable Costs	Total Costs
0	0	0	0
1	20	20	20
2	60	40	30
3	110	50	36.6
4	180	70	47.5
5	210	30	42
6	232	22	34
7	238	6	34
8	242	6	30.25
9	245	3	27.2
10	247	2	24.7

Figure 4.1

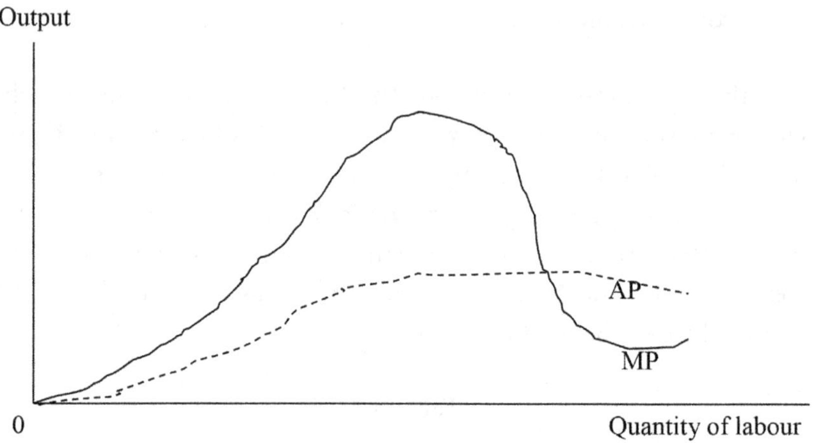

From **Figure 4.1** it can be seen that the amount of additional output you get from each additional unit of input decreases as you use more and more of the input.

Question 1

(b) Does the law of diminishing returns apply to all factors of production?

MODEL ANSWER:

The law of diminishing returns applies to all factors of production. It operates whenever some factors are fixed and others are variable. For example, in factories the size of the plant may be fixed and it may be essential to vary the level of output by changing the quantities of a variable input such as labour.

Up to a point, the level of income will increase (since total output increases). However, as more workers are added, diminishing returns set in and, once the factory gets overstaffed, inefficiency may result from overcrowding. The marginal product will fall as a result.

Question 2

(a) *Despite the advantages to be gained from large size, small firms continue to exist and operate. Using suitable examples, explain the reason for this.*

MODEL ANSWER:

Despite the advantages to be gained from increasing size, a large number of small firms continue to exist and operate. There are many sound reasons to explain this.

* *Justification of the size of demand for one final product:* Large scale methods of production are not economically efficient unless justified by the size of demand for the final product. Many small firms continue to exist because the market they supply is relatively small. In such cases, the size of the production unit will also be small. Examples of such markets are linked to luxury goods such as fur coats, sports cars and quality jewellery which only a relatively small number of wealthy people can afford.

* *Transport costs:* bulky commodities (such as bricks, cement, bags of maize) can be quite expensive to transport over long distances. In which case, markets for such commodities are likely to be local, rather than national, and therefore small.

* *Personal attention to customers is an essential part of the service:* in some industries, firms remain small in order to provide personal and direct services to their clients. Examples of such industries can be found in medicine, law, and hairdressing.

* *Product differentiation:* may split up the market artificially into small sizes, with small firms serving these individual markets.

* *Consumers demand a variety of product patterns and designs.* The demand for a particular pattern or design of an item may be quite small. Examples are to be found in the case of highly specialized

machine tools which are often individually designed and in footwear, jewellery and clothing.

* *Other factors:*

Even when the size of the market is large, factors on the supply side may prevent the growth of firms. For example, government may prevent mergers between firms to avoid the emergence of monopolies and difficulties in raising capital may prevent other firms from expanding.

As the firm grows the task of management becomes more challenging and complex. With increasing size, the task of coordination and control of the firm's activities could become increasingly complex, whereas for smaller firms the task of management is relatively easy.

Finally, consistent with the factor just mentioned, a small owner may not have the ability to supervise a large firm, or he may prefer a quiet life as opposed to the long hours and extra problems that come with increasing size.

Question 3

(a) Describe a firm's profit maximization condition.

MODEL ANSWER

Under normal business conditions, a typical firm's objective is to maximize profits or minimize losses, but this is of particular concern when the business climate is poor. Here profit (π) is defined as total revenue **(TR)** minus total costs **(TC)**. Whatever the business climate, the question that is always uppermost in the firm's mind is: will it make or lose money? What level of output must it maintain to make a profit? Or, given existing business conditions, is it at risk of losing money? At the very least, the firm's goal must be to attain a *break-even* point where: **TR** = **TC**.

To arrive at an optimal decision, the firm puts together the *cost* information and the *revenue* information and then reviews both. In a perfectly competitive market and to get the maximum level of profits, the firm will continue to produce as long as *marginal revenue* (**MR**) *is greater than or equal to marginal cost* (**MC**). This means that the *profit maximizing quantity* (output) for the firm occurs when marginal revenue is equal to marginal cost (or **MR** = **MC**). This is illustrated in **Figure 4.2** below.

Figure 4.2

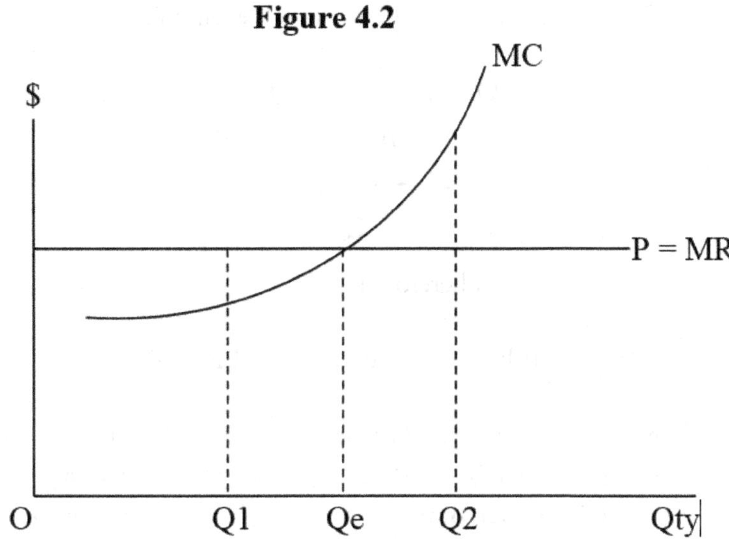

Where: Qe is the profit-maximizing (π) output.

In **Figure 4.2** Qe is the profit-maximizing level of output. At Q1, which is below Qe, the firm would lose revenue. And at Q2, the firm would be producing units that earn less in revenue than they cost to produce overall. The firm loses money at Q2.

The logic behind this analysis is simple: every unit that generates more in revenue than it costs benefits the firm. At Qe (the profit-maximization point), each unit *adds more* to the firm's revenue than it costs to produce. Note that Qe is also the loss-minimizing level of output.

To determine if the firm is making or losing money, we need to know the firm's average cost (**AC**) at output Qe. Bearing in mind that the firm earns a normal profit, it would be true to say that all information costs have been taken into full account when the total revenue (**TR**) of the firm is equal to its total costs (**TC**) of production. But we also know that total revenue (**TR**) = unit price (**P**) x quantity (**Q**) and that total costs (**TC**) = average unit cost (**AC**) x quantity. Thus, we can then calculate **P** when **TR** = **TC**.

That is: when **TR** = **TC** (the break-even point).

Or P x Q = AC x Q

$$P = \frac{AC \times Q}{Q}$$

Therefore P = AC

Note that: Profit (π) is defined as: **TR – TC**.

Hence, a firm makes a *normal profit* when the ***price*** (**P**) of its products is **equal to** its average costs (**AC**), i.e., **P** = **AC**. It earns an *economic profit* when **P ≥ AC**, i.e., price is **greater than** average cost. It incurs an *economic loss* when **P ≤ AC**, i.e., is **less than** average costs. Again bear in mind that average costs (**AC**) = **AFC** + **AVC** (that is adding average fixed costs and average variable costs together). These conditions are illustrated in **Figure 4.3.**

Figure 4.3

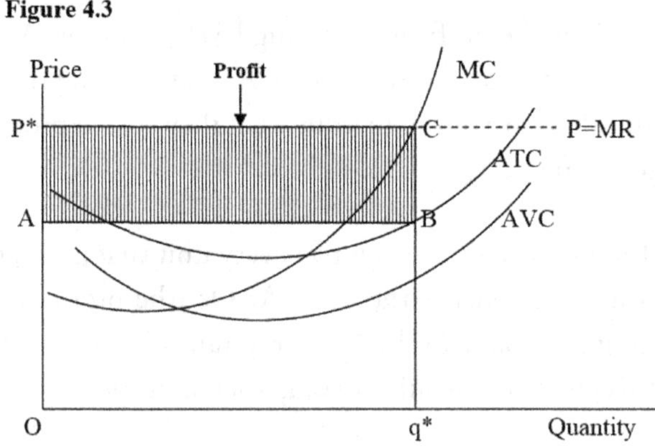

Profit (π) is the shaded area, which is the difference between TR and TC.

Question 4

(a) *Using suitable examples explain the difference between fixed costs and variable costs. Explain how fixed and variable costs affect a firm's choice of optimal output both in the short run and the long run.*

MODEL ANSWER:

Fixed costs are those that do not change as the level of total output changes. By their very nature, fixed costs are associated with a firm's plant and machinery and must be paid even if the firm is producing nothing at all or is at a production standstill of zero output. Money spent on machinery is sometimes referred to as capital costs. Examples of fixed costs are: rent, interest on borrowed money and insurance.

Variable costs are those costs that increase with as the level of output grows. These costs are zero if you produce nothing. Examples are: raw material costs, energy, transport costs and wages. Variable costs are subject to the law of diminishing returns. Variable costs, also known as operating costs, are thus under the control of the firm while fixed costs are not. Total costs are the costs (both fixed and variable) incurred by the firm in its production process. Thus, **TC = FC + VC**.

Table 4.2 and **Figure 4.4** illustrate the two concepts.

Table 4.2

Total Product	Fixed Costs	Variable Costs	Total Costs
1	100	20	120
2	100	40	140
3	100	80	180
4	100	140	240
5	100	160	260

6	100	175	275
7	100	182	282
8	100	185	285
9	100	187	287
10	100	188	288

Figure 4.4

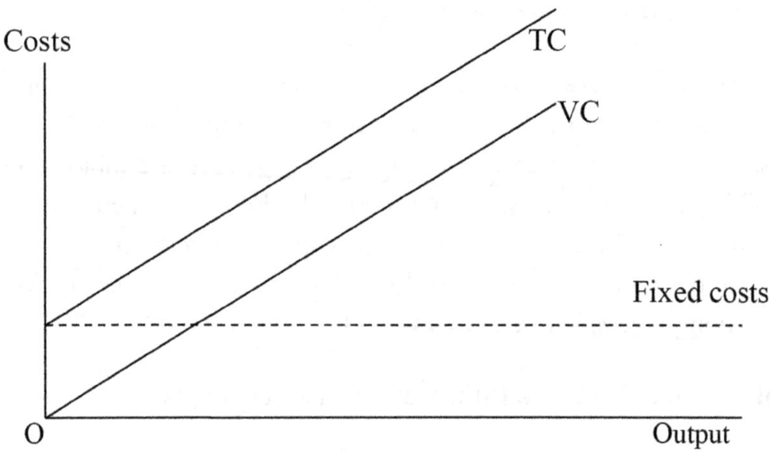

Question 5

(a) Distinguish between (i) short-run and (ii) long-run costs.

MODEL ANWER:

The firm's short-run costs endure or are current to the end of the firm's fixed contract. That is the period when some factors of production are fixed. The firm has to meet all its fixed cost commitments until they either expire or are completely covered. Costs such as rent have to be paid regardless. So the thing that is of particular concern when dealing with a plant of fixed-size is its variable costs. Conversely, long-run costs begin when the short-run period ends because at that point, a firm, if it so wishes, can cease business operations and exit the industry.

In the long-run, both fixed costs and variable costs are to be taken into consideration when making decisions. That is, all of the production resources, including those that are fixed, can be varied or adjusted. For example, rent can become larger if the facility is expanded; just as the firm can borrow more money to hire more workers if it expects an increase in demand or an expansion of the market for its products.

An increase in wages increases the industry's long run costs of production at every level of output.

There are several reasons why a firm may go out of business. The decision may be due to social factors like the poor health or death of the owners or it may be as a result of other factors such as the unavailability of raw materials, poor equipment, lack of working capital and so on. But the biggest *incentive* for a firm to stay in business is ***profits***. Unless it is a charitable organization, in which case priority is put on non-profit or social values. And the biggest *hindrance* to a firm continuing in business is unsustainable ***excessive losses***. When you walk along a street or industrial district and see many "out of business" signs those are indicative of hard decisions those firms had to make to cut their losses. Such a situation is hinged on this single critical question: when does a firm ***close down***?

(i) Short-run shut down condition.

A loss-making firm closes down production as soon as the amount it would make by closing shop is *less than* the amount of loss that it would incur by continuing to produce goods until its *fixed costs* contract expires.

Recall that: TC = FC + VC

Where: Fixed costs (FC) are those incurred even at zero output (i.e., when the firm is producing nothing). The logic here is that, if the firm cannot make a profit, the losses it suffers must at least be *less than* the fixed costs

(FC) it has to honor even if it is doing nothing (at zero output). **Figure 4.5** below helps to illustrate this.

Figure 4.5

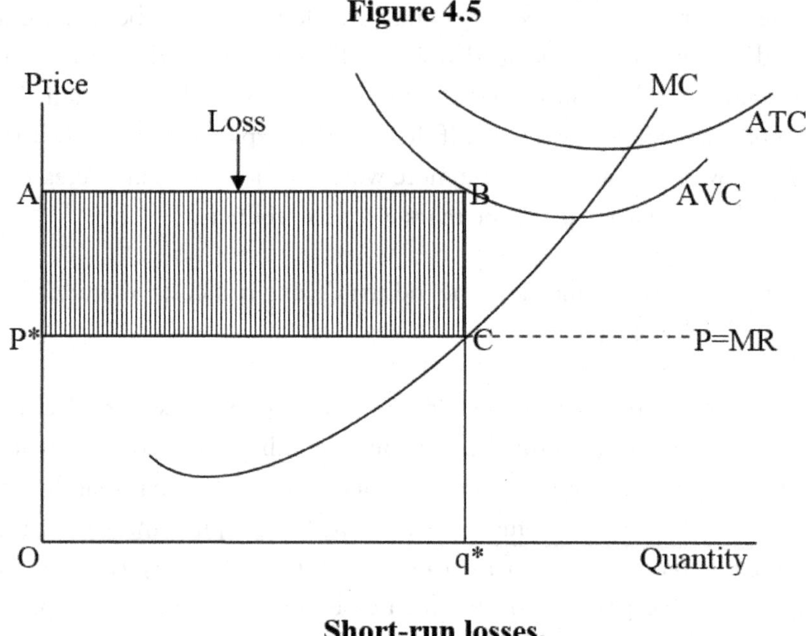

Short-run losses.

In **Figure 4.5** when price (p*) is low such that the marginal revenue (P =MR) curve *intersects* the marginal cost (MC) curve *below* the average variable cost (AVC) curve, the firm makes losses. At this optimal output level (q*), total revenue (TR = p* x q*) is less than or cannot cover variable costs – which is represented by rectangle OABq*. Therefore, at this point (in the short-run), it is best to shut down immediately and produce nothing.

Short-run losses (**shut-down**) is the shaded area P*ABC in the diagram. The firm shuts down quickly when the loss it would make by closing shop is *less than* the amount of loss it would suffer if it continued to produce up to the point where it no longer had fixed costs. This means the firm's TR is less than even its variable costs (VC), let alone its TC. Therefore it is better for the firm to stop producing to eliminate variable costs. If the firm produces nothing, then the only loss it incurs are fixed costs (FC).

As an example, suppose a firm produces copper output q*, with its fixed costs (FC) set at $2000/Mt, its total revenue (TR) at price p* amounting to only $800/Mt, but its variable cost (VC) reaching $1000/Mt. This would generate a loss in variable costs of $200/Mt ($1000-$800) – which must be added to the fixed costs (FC), since TC = FC + VC. Then the firm would lose in total $2200 ($2000 + $200). But if the firm were to shut down operations (it saves on variable costs), then it would lose ***only*** $2000 (the fixed costs), which is lower than $2200.

(ii) Long-run shut down condition.

In the long-run, this situation occurs when a loss-making firm is better off waiting until its fixed costs (FC) commitments have expired before closing down. That is, the firm acts when its total revenue (TR) *exceeds* its variable costs (VC) but is *less than* its total costs (TC). See **Figure 4.6** below.

Figure 4.6

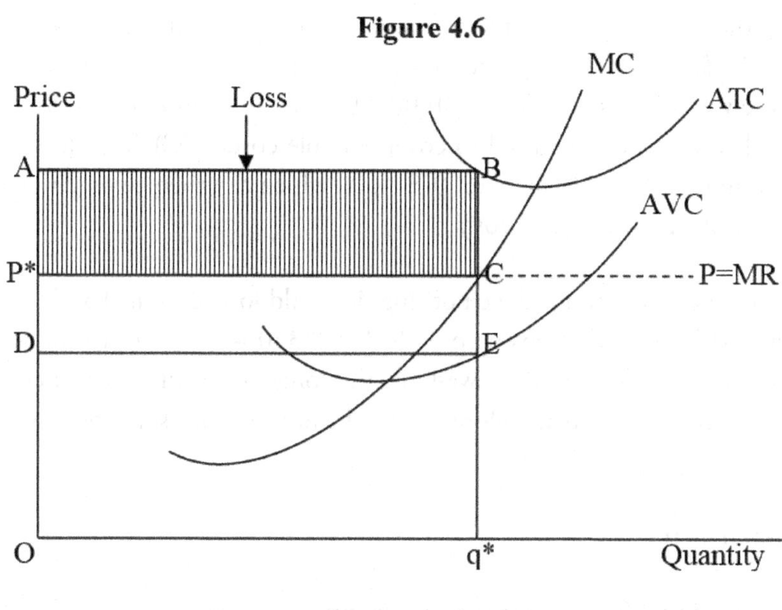

Long-run losses

In **Figure 4.6**, the optimal level at point C, where P = MR line crosses the marginal cost (MC) curve *lies above the bottom* of the average variable costs (AVC), but *below the bottom* of average total costs (ATC) curve. In this case: the firm's total revenue (TR) = (p* x q*) – represented by the rectangle Op*Cq* -- is *greater than* its variable costs (VC), represented by rectangle ODEq*. The excess variable costs (VC), can be used to pay off part of the firm's fixed costs (FC).

Long-run losses (**shut-down**) is shaded area P*ABC, since TC ≥ TR. Area P*DEC shows revenue sufficient enough to cover the firm's variable costs (VC) and part of its fixed costs (FC). In this case, when TR is at least *greater than* variable costs (VC), even though it is *less than* TC, no decision is taken to shut down immediately. Since the total revenue (TR) is more than variable costs (VC), part of that revenue earned can be used to pay off part of the firm's fixed costs (FC) – a better scenario.

If the firm shuts down and produces nothing, all of its fixed costs (FC) would be lost, but that is a position that would leave it worse off.

Using the copper example above: suppose at output q*, fixed costs (FC) are again $2000/Mt, but the total revenue (TR) at price p* is $1600/Mt and the variable costs (VC) are $1400/Mt. The first $1400 of the $1600 in total revenues can be used to cover variable costs (VC). This leaves a surplus in revenues of $200 ($1600-$1400), which can then be used to pay off some of the firm's fixed costs.

If the firm chooses to produce nothing, it would lose all of its fixed costs ($2000/Mt) rather than losing only $1800 ($3400-$1600) if it produces q* output. In this case, firm waits in the long-run until its fixed-costs commitments have ended, before exiting the industry (i.e. shutting down).

Question 6

(a) Analyze the effect on long run costs in an industry when:
(i) there is introduction of new technology;
(ii) there is an increase in wages.

MODEL ANSWER:

The short run in the theory of the firm is defined as that period when some factors of production, such as rent, are fixed. As explained earlier, in the short run the level of fixed costs, which have to be paid regardless, do not affect the firm's choice of optimal output, only its variable costs matter at that point. The long run corresponds to that period of time when all costs, whether fixed or variable, can be adjusted. During this time the firm can vary even its plant size in order to determine what is optimal.

(i) An improvement in technology is beneficial to the extent that it lowers the firm's costs of production. This means that at every level of output the costs of production are lower.
(ii) An increase in wages increases the industry's long run costs of production at every level of output.

Thus in **Figure 4.7** an increase in wages would shift the AC0 to AC1 and MC0 to MC1 while an improvement in technology would shift the cost curves in the opposite direction.

Figure 4.7

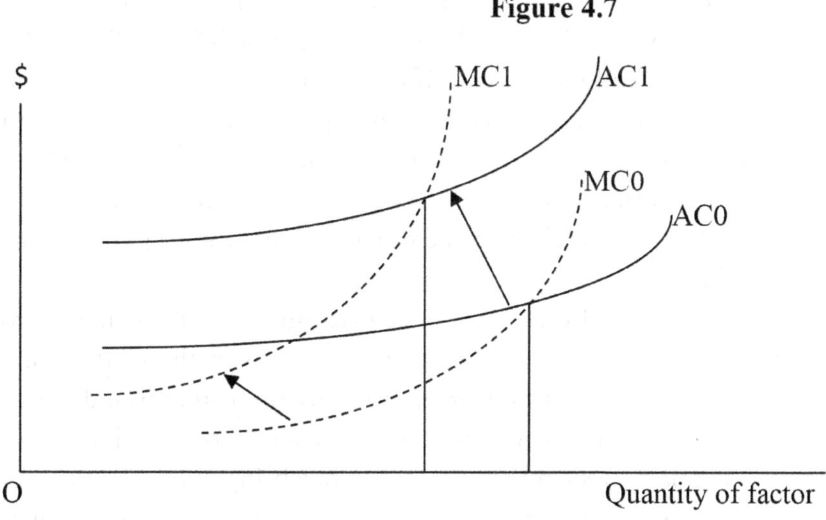

Question 7

(a) Discuss price discrimination and state some of its conditions.

MODEL ANSWER: I

Price Discrimination: Background

Price discrimination is the selling of the *same* commodity to *different buyers* at *different prices.*

Conditions necessary for price discrimination are:

- There must be a separation of markets preventing buyers from one market re-selling the item to another (i.e., no arbitrage).
- The seller must possess some monopolistic power in at least one market. Under competitive conditions, this means that prices will be driven down to the level of costs in all markets.
- Buyers in different markets must have different levels of income and elasticity of demand for the commodity.
- A monopolist who price discriminates will set output for each market where: MC = MR in that market or MC = MRx = MRy (where x and y represent different markets). The sale price will be higher in a market where elasticity of demand is low than where it is high. This permits the firm to take advantage of the fact that in one market consumers are prepared to pay more for the same good than in the other – without losing sales in the other market.
- Also, as noted earlier, for price discrimination in the market to be possible, there must exist imperfections in the market. In a perfectly competitive market, price discrimination would not be possible for mainly two reasons: 1) if competitors could influence the pricing system (instead of everyone being price-takers); or, 2) if customers who are offered lower prices could resell to customers who are offered higher prices.
- In addition, firms must be aware that if this practice is introduced, it would not cause any consumer resentment thereby affecting

market shares and hence profits. Also, price discrimination should not be based on differences in the costs of production.

- These conditions taken together will ensure that a producer can *maximize profits by charging different prices.* A price discriminating monopolist will set output for each market where MC = MR in that particular market.
- A good example where price discrimination conditions are met is in the *airline industry.* A small number of airlines dominate the industry, giving them *market power.* Different travelers are likely to have different *elasticities of demand,* hence price sensitivity. Due to modern computer technology, market segmentation and monitoring become easy. And since possibilities of *re-selling* can therefore be made difficult, if not impossible, price discrimination becomes feasible.

Question 7

(b) Can you illustrate price discrimination with examples?

MODEL ANSWER: II

Price discrimination is the practice whereby different buyers are charged different prices for the same commodity or service. A price setter, such as a monopolist, has the ability to price-discriminate for its products. A few examples might help illustrate this concept:

* Cinemas sometimes charge lower admission fees for children than for adults.

* Some firms sell goods at a lower price in foreign markets than in the domestic market.

* Doctors sometimes charge different fees to patients depending on the patient's income status.

* In some countries, telephone charges vary depending on the time of day.

Question 7

(c) Is there a rationale for price discrimination in economic analysis?

MODEL ANSWER: III

Yes, in economic analysis this is associated with the demand curve and with consumer surplus. For example, depending on the price of the product or service, consumers can utilize a part of or the whole portion of consumer surplus. It is a question of maximizing consumption. Using a demand curve in a diagram, it can be illustrated that *consumers' willingness to pay* for a product or service provides a rationale for price discrimination. **See Figure 4.8.**

Figure 4.8

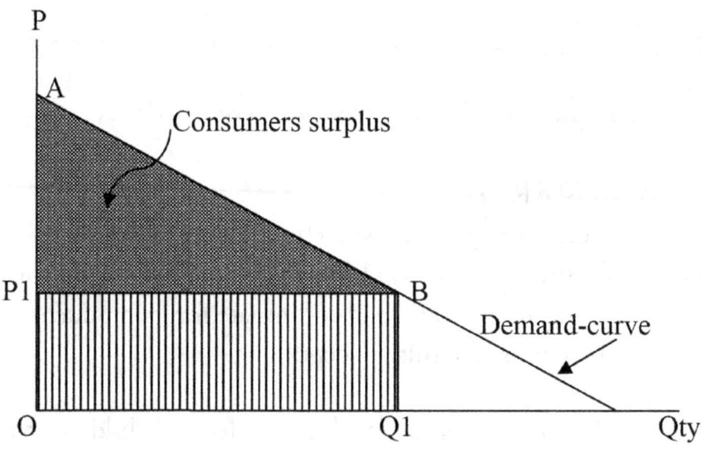

Demand, Willingness to pay & Price Discrimination

In **Figure 4.8**, let us assume that P1 is the price of a product and Q1 is the quantity demanded at that price. The assumption here with a demand curve is that all units of a product are sold at whatever price exists in the market. From the Figure we can see that the total amount consumers are *willing to pay* for Q1 units of output, rather than go without it, is area OABQ1. But the amount they *actually pay* or spend on the product at price P1 is only the area OP1BQ1. Therefore the difference is *consumers' surplus* is the area ABP1.

Hence, with a first-degree price discrimination strategy in operation, firms can convert this consumer surplus (area ABP1) into revenue. Firms take note of the total amount consumers are willing to pay for all units, which represents the *marginal benefit* or dollar-value consumers attach to each additional unit of the good/product; the area underneath the demand-curve up to quantity Q1.

Question 7

(d) State in details the necessary conditions for price discrimination to be:
(i) possible,
(ii) profitable.

MODEL ANSWER II:

(i) For price discrimination to be possible there must exist *imperfections* in the market. In a perfectly competitive market price discrimination would not be possible because customers who are buying at lower prices would resell to those customers who are paying higher prices. Imperfect market conditions will allow a producer to maximize profits by charging different prices in different segments of the market.

It should be possible for the producer to *separate the market* into two distinct segments such that one group of consumers cannot resell to another (i.e., no arbitrage).

There must be significant differences between the different classes of consumers in their *willingness to pay* for the item. Explained another way, this condition says that the elasticity of demand for buyers in each market segment should be different. This will enable the producer to maximize profits by charging different prices in different segments of the market.

Finally, it should be possible for the producer to *enforce* his pricing arrangements in the different segments of the market.

(ii) The condition for maximum profits under price discrimination is

MC=MRA=MRB

Where MRA and MRB are the marginal revenues in the two submarkets A and B, respectively.

To achieve this, the price discriminator will always set the price higher in the market with the lower elasticity of demand.

This analysis is illustrated in **Figure 4.9** for two submarkets A and B. **Figures 4.9 (a)** and **4.9 (b)** show the demand and marginal revenue curves for the two submarkets. The curve MRT is the *sum* of the MR curves of the two firms. The equilibrium or profit maximizing level of output will be achieved at the point OP* in **Figure 4.9 (c)** where MC=MRT. Since, in this case, demand is less elastic in A than in B, price is higher and quantity lower in A than in B.

Figure 4.9

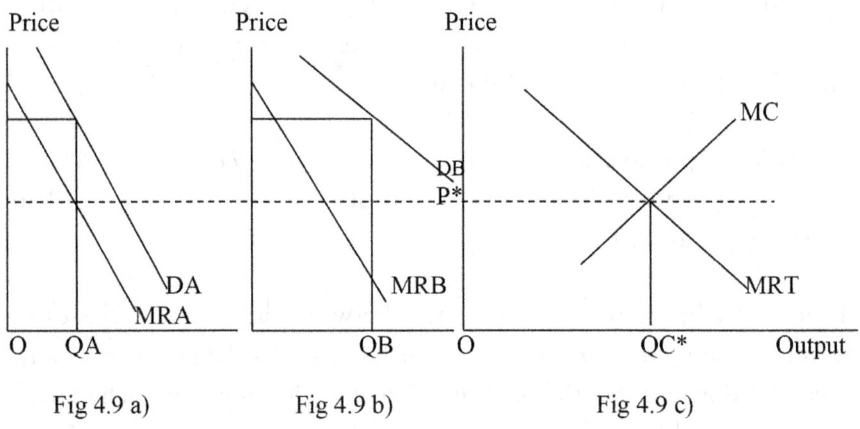

Fig 4.9 a) Fig 4.9 b) Fig 4.9 c)

Question 7

(e) Can price discrimination ever benefit the consumer?

MODEL ANSWER:

Under price discrimination both levels of profit and output will be higher than for a non-discriminating monopoly. This has two important implications for consumer welfare:

* It will make it possible for the firm to supply a particular market which under non-discrimination would not be profitable. For example, in the absence of discrimination it may not be profitable for a firm to supply a particular region at a certain price. However, it could well be that consumers in that region are willing to pay a higher price in order to obtain the commodity or service.

* Under price discrimination it may also be possible for the firm to supply a commodity or service where no single price would cover the firm's total costs of production.

Question 8

(a) Briefly discuss the tenets/principles behind perfect competition.

MODEL ANSWER:

In a market economy, there are several kinds of *market structures* – the most prominent one being *perfect competition.* Other structures representing imperfect completion are: monopoly, monopolistic competition, and oligopoly.

In *perfect competition* the main features are: *large number* of independent buyers and sellers; producers' *products are identical*; *no barriers to entry*; existence of perfect knowledge and every consumer is *a price-taker* (i.e., demand curve is horizontal or infinitely elastic).

- In the **short run**, the condition for a perfect competition is: Set MR = P = MC (a so-called MC-price setting).
  If P ≥ AC, the firm is making profits, where profit per unit is the difference between the price and average cost (AC). If P is below the *lowest point* of the average cost (AC) curve: instead of maximizing profits, the firm would aim at lowering losses. Hence, in general, firms aim for covering ALL variable costs (VC) plus a bit for fixed costs (FC). In the long run, the firm would of course close if losses persist. As loss-making firms exit the industry, this causes the price to rise until the remaining firms *break even*. New entrants come in when the price becomes too good (P ≥ AVC) to be ignored, because it is creating *abnormal profits*, which attracts many would-be profiteers whose oversupply of the product causes its price to fall once more.
- In the **long-run,** firms set price (P) = (AC) average cost and profit zero (i.e., $\pi = 0$). Hence:

  [P = MC = MR = AC = AR]

where *marginal revenue* (MR) is the additional revenue from selling one additional unit, which also happens to be the price (P) of the commodity. As an example: let *maize price per tin be $5*. The total revenue (TR = p x q) for selling 100 tins is $500 (i.e., 100 x $5). TR for selling 101 tins is $505. Therefore the MR = $5, which is the additional revenue from selling 1 additional unit. But since this is also the price of maize per tin, hence MR = P.

Given the fact that *marginal cost* (MC) is the rate at which total costs (TC) is changing, and since marginal revenue (MR) is the rate at which total revenue (TR) is changing, ***equilibrium*** occurs when MC = MR (the point where profits can be maximized).

Consequently: (a) If MR ≥ MC, the firm makes a profit by increasing its output. For example if MC = $3 and MR = $3 at that point the *last unit* produced would add $3 to revenues and $3 to costs; i.e., total profits would be *as large as possible.*

(b) If MC ≥ MR, the firm could increase its profits only by *reducing* its output. For example, if MC = $3.50 and MR = $3, i.e., we sell a good for $3 which costs us $3.50 to produce, this creates a tendency to reduce output. Therefore, to maximize profits, the firm's ***marginal benefits*** must be equal to ***marginal costs.*** So you aim to produce at the point where MR = MC.

In summary: when costs vary with output, to *maximize profits* requires the output level where the difference between total revenue (TR) and total costs (TC) *is greatest*; i.e., (TR – TC) = Maximum Profit.

Question 9

(a) Explain briefly how prices and output are determined by:
(i) a perfectly competitive firm;
(ii) a monopolist; and also
(iii) how the consumer is affected in each case?

MODEL ANSWER:

(i) ***Perfect competition*** describes a theoretical market structure which is characterized by a large number of independent buyers and sellers, a homogeneous (or identical) commodity, freedom of entry and exit of new firms into the industry and perfect knowledge among all market participants. No single firm or buyer can influence the price. They are all price-takers – taking the price as given. A price-taker is also by definition a quantity adjuster. For example, a firm can sell as much as it wants at a prevailing price. These characteristics ensure that the firm will face a perfectly elastic demand curve for its product.

In the *short run*, the perfectly competitive firm maximizes profits by equating MC=MR. This is illustrated in **Figure 4.10**. The firm will produce output Q1 at a price P1. At this level of output the firm has no incentive to produce any other quantity. In the short run, under perfect competition, the perfectly competitive firm earns abnormal profits. These are indicated by the shaded area in the diagram. Because the firm faces a perfectly elastic demand curve for its product and the price level is given (meaning, it is a price-taker), the equilibrium condition is given as p=MC=MC=AR.

Figure 4.10

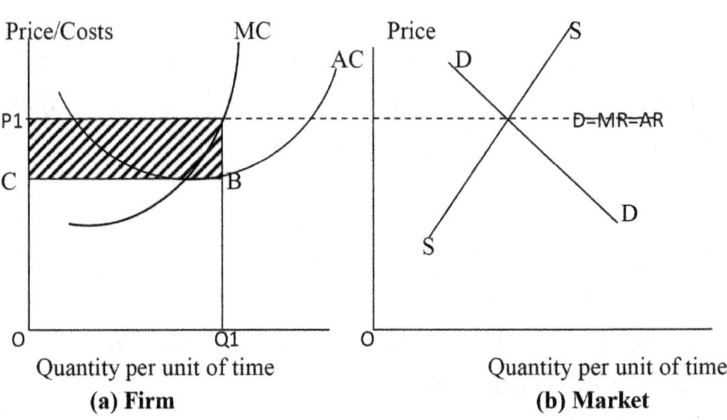

(a) Firm **(b) Market**

The *long run* equilibrium in the theory of the firm is achieved after a sufficient period of time has passed to permit any existing participating firms wishing to leave the industry to do so and allow potential new entrants to join. In the long run, new firms will be attracted to the industry by the *abnormal profits* being earned. This means that at any given price, more will be supplied. As a result, the tendency of the market will be to bid the price downwards with old and new firms alike adjusting their levels of output accordingly. The increased competition reduces the abnormal profits and all firms will end up again earning only *normal profits.*

The long run equilibrium conditions for a perfectly competitive firm are illustrated in **Figure 4.11**. From the diagram we can see that the price equals the minimum average cost which indicates that only normal profits are being earned in the long run under perfect competition and is represented by the equation:

$$p=MC=MR=AC=AR$$

Ultimately, the firm will set p=AC and profit (π)=0.

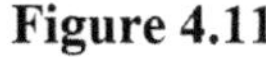

Figure 4.11

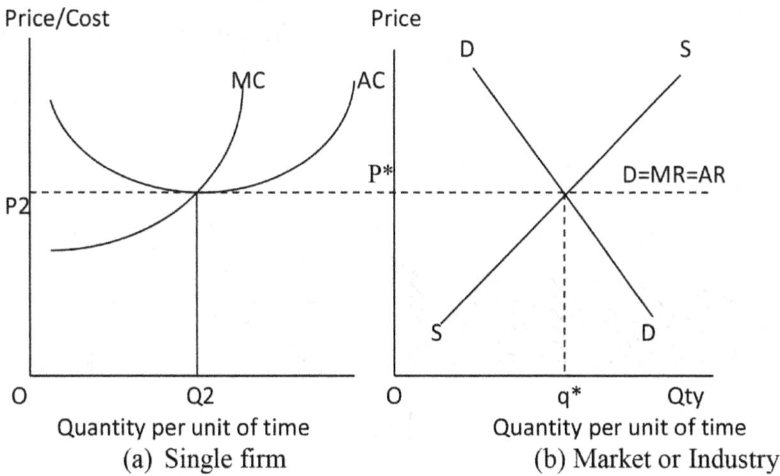

(a) Single firm (b) Market or Industry

(ii) The opposite of perfect competition is monopoly. A ***monopoly*** is a sole supplier of a commodity or service and as such he can control his price or his output but not both. As a single seller in a one firm industry, the firm exercises substantial control over the industry (either control over its supply or some key production input). And usually the product has no close substitutes. Entry is barred. Monopoly provides some latitude through price-discrimination. A monopoly is an example of *imperfect competition*. Good examples are: local gas or electricity companies, or public utilities such as sewer and water companies. Monopoly differs from perfect competition in that under perfect competition the firm is a ***price-taker*** and quantity-adjuster. Since there is no price discrimination, a monopolist lowers price to increase its sales; or it charges high prices to make monopoly profits.

To maintain monopoly profits (π), the company lowers price to increase its sales or charges high prices for its output. Left alone, a monopolist would tend to produce less, below socially desirable levels. That is why there is a need for governments to regulate monopolies. Because, without regulation or public control, and in order to maximize profits, a monopolist would simply restrict output below a socially desirable level. Regulation is done through, say, anti-trust laws or the setting up of anti-monopoly commissions.

Figure 4.12

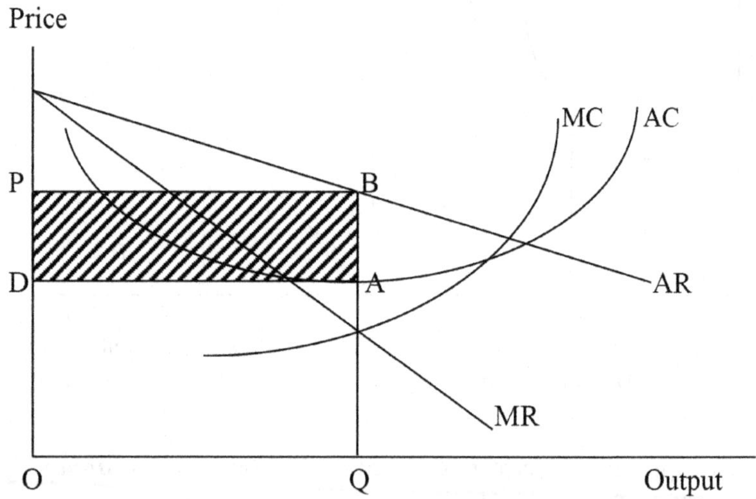

To maximize profit the monopolist sets MC=MR. This equilibrium condition is illustrated in **Figure 4.12**. From the diagram we can see that the monopolist is making *abnormal profits* because the price line lies above the minimum point of the AC curve. Under perfect competition, the abnormal profits would attract new firms in the industry. Under monopoly, the entry of new firms is prevented by the existence of various barriers to entry such as patents, economies of scale (such as in the case of natural monopolies) and so on. Due to the existence of economies of scale, the firm's average costs (AC) are so low, smaller firms find it virtually impossible to compete with the dominant giant.

(iii) Under ***perfect competition*** the level of prices is determined by free market forces without any interference on the part of the producer. As already noted, the firm under perfect competition is a *price-taker* – it takes the price as given and then adjusts quantity accordingly. Furthermore, under perfect competition, long run equilibrium is achieved when price equals minimum average cost of production so that the *consumer is not exploited*. On the other hand, under a monopoly, the price is greater than the minimum average cost both in the short and long run. Hence, the consumer is exploited. The consumer purchasing a monopoly product pays a price that exceeds the opportunity cost of the resources used in producing that commodity.

Some monopolies fall under imperfect competition. Under *imperfect competition*, for a given technology, prices are higher and outputs are larger.

Large firms exploit economies of large-scale production and are responsible for much of the industrial innovation occurring as opposed to a perfect competition situation where no firm is large enough to affect the market price on its own. A good illustration of imperfect competition can be observed in the United States following World War II when some firms like Ford Motors, GM, Alcoa and others grew so big they had some control over the prices of their outputs. The same case could be made for Toyota and Honda in Japan.

Varieties of imperfect competition, depending on patterns of competition, can be characterized as: monopoly; oligopoly; and monopolistic competition.

There are other aspects of ***monopoly behavior*** which have a bearing on consumer welfare. In particular, the following should be noted:

- The monopolist can practice price discrimination, given the full extent of his power over the pricing system. By so doing, he forces one group of consumers to subsidize another. It can be objected that the monopolist has no right to decide which group of consumers should subsidize another.

- The quality of products under monopoly is likely to be inferior due to the absence of competitive pressures. For that same reason, the monopolist has little incentive to apply cost minimizing methods of production so that his prices will tend to remain high. Under perfect competition firms are under pressure to reduce prices, due to the existence of competitive pressures.

Against this, it should be noted that prices under monopoly will tend to be more stable than under prefect competition. Furthermore, under perfect competition a firm may find itself incurring large expenditures in advertising. These are costs which may eventually have to be borne by the consumer.

Question 10

(a) *The assumptions underlying perfect competition are very unlikely to be satisfied. "Discuss".*

MODEL ANSWER:

Perfect competition describes a theoretical market situation in which competition among firms reaches its maximum level of impact. The model of perfect competition is based on a number of assumptions, the most important of which are mentioned and discussed below.

* *Large number of buyers and sellers:* because of this, the individual firm's supply only accounts for a small proportion of the total industry output. Thus, any variation in total supply will not have a significant effect on the price of the product. Because the seller will be faced with a perfectly elastic demand curve for his product.

Similarly, purchasers of goods and factors of production are faced with a perfectly elastic supply curve. On the production side, a single producer can increase the demand for a factor of production but this will not have a significant effect on the price of that factor.

* *Homogeneous products:* All products are assumed homogeneous (that is, alike in every respect) so buyers are indifferent as to which product they purchase.

* *Perfect knowledge:* perfect knowledge is assumed to exist between buyers and sellers. This means that market participants know exactly what prices are being asked in other sections of the market and producers know the profits that are being earned by their competitors.

* *Perfect mobility:* all factors of production are assumed to move from one industry to another in response to changing expectations of the rewards to be earned.

* *Freedom of entry/exit:* there is freedom of entry of new firms in the industry. This means that firms can move in and out of the industry in response to changing profit expectations.

But in real life, it is obvious that these conditions will not be satisfied. To understand why, let us examine each of the assumptions in turn.

* *Many buyers and many sellers:* in reality, this condition is not generally satisfied and we find that there is sometimes a few (oligopoly) or even one seller of a commodity (monopoly). Under such conditions firms have some degree of control over their prices and outputs.

* *Homogenous commodity:* this condition is also not satisfied in reality because firms may differentiate their products through branding and packaging.

* *Perfect knowledge:* in the real world there are restrictions to the flow of information. Furthermore, information may be costly to obtain, therefore this condition is not likely to be satisfied either.

* *Perfect mobility of factors of production:* factors of production are not perfectly mobile as assumed in the theory of perfect competition. Barriers to factor mobility may arise for reasons such as the lack of information, costs of moving from one location to another, and differences in cost associated with siting firms in different locations.

* *Freedom of entry and exit of new firms:* this final assumption is not likely to be satisfied either. Freedom of entry or exit may be restricted by firms with excessive market power. Such firms may create barriers to new entrants by using their considerable resources to maintain their lead in the industry and limit the distribution of profits to existing competitors.

* Even so, economists find the model of perfect competition useful for two main reasons:

    - The model is a useful approximation to real world markets. Original assumptions can be modified to make the model conform more closely to real world market conditions. In this way, we are able to gain a better understanding of real world markets.

    - The model gives a useful indication of the conditions necessary to achieve economic efficiency. For instance, to promote economic efficiency, the government can introduce measures to improve the flow of information or improve the efficiency of labour.

Thus while perfect competition is not likely to be achieved in practice, knowledge of how a perfectly competitive market operates can enhance our understanding of real world markets and provide guidelines for industrial action.

Question 11

(a) What is a monopoly market? Can you clearly explain its main features?

MODEL ANSWER:

Monopoly is a market with only *one (firm) supplier*; there are *no competitors* in the industry. The main features of this situation can be described in this manner: the firm is motivated by profits and the limit for its production is reached when marginal revenue (MR) = (MC) the marginal cost. The firm *stands alone* and *barriers* prevent new firms from entering. The actions of the monopolist itself affect the market price of its output. Therefore, it *is not a price taker*. But a monopolist faces a *downward-sloping* marginal revenue (MR) curve as opposed to *a horizontal* one (MR) faced by competitive firms.

A *discriminating monopolist* charges different prices for the same product to different consumers. A ***monopsony*** has a greater impact on market price because this is a market with only one buyer of the item sold. In that market, when the buyer purchases an extra unit, market demand increases perceptibly and the market price rises. Hence, in some markets you can see why it could pay to restrict demand.

Monopolistic Competition – is a case when there are a large number of monopoly-like firms. Examples are: cereals firms, soft drinks companies and automobile manufacturers. Relying on non-price competition, they *partially differentiate* their products to have some control over price. Products are not identical like in perfect competition. The idea is to protectively set one's product apart from competitors, isolating it from price competition, until the firm becomes *a price-maker.* That is, within limits, this *monopolistic power* enables the firm to control/or set prices. There are no barriers to entry in this particular case.

But differentiation comes at a cost through: engineering costs, market research and advertisement. If this action cannot bring the desired results, firms then resort to buying up competition, amalgamation and/or the creation of mergers.

Hence, in the short run, a *monopolistic competitor* can earn *economic profits* greater than even in a pure competitive environment. In the long run, however, more firms eventually enter to share the *abnormal profits* available, just as they would in a situation of perfect competition. The key with these firms is that each has its own *special ambience* or *individual branding.* Examples are, Blue Jeans firms like Levi's, Rider or Calvin Klein, or Guess – which differentiates their products by style. Other examples could be: Chinese or Italian restaurants, ethnic beauty salons or barber shops. Advertisement and other non-price competitive features are also important ingredients for success with these types of firms. Excess capacity is another common feature with these firms.

Question 11

(b) Can you discuss the benefits and evils of monopoly?

MODEL ANSWER:

(i) ***Benefits*** of some monopolies include the following:

- Monopolies encourage innovation: Because patents give owners or investors some monopolistic power and the exclusive right to market their inventions for 20 years, this encourages innovation because more money and effort is spent on research and development (R & D). Rights are granted to avoid copycats flooding the market and thereby reducing incentives for more inventions.

- To cut redundancy, some natural monopolies like Natural Gas/ Utilities/Water or Fiber-Optic internet access are preferred. Otherwise, competition would cause annoying redundancies. Imagine providing many different sets of optics or pipe lines to a neighborhood; it is better to have one supplier than many.

- Monopolies also help to keep costs low; such is the case for natural monopoly industries which allow for economies of scale. If one industry can produce output at a lower average cost (AC) per unit -- for example, electric power generation or water utility – this keeps prices low. These benefits are realized when monopolies are regulated or supported by government.

(ii) ***Evils (Disadvantages)*** associated with monopolies include the following:

- Some monopolies are considered socially harmful because of their tendency to produce less output than would be done by firms in perfect competition. For this reason some monopolies are illegal.

- Also, since a monopoly sells its output at a higher price than the market price that would result from competition, consumers are penalized.

- In addition, monopoly output is produced *less efficiently* and at *a higher cost* than it would in a competitive industry, given the existence of a secure market for the product. This occurs because for a low output, marginal revenue (MR) is greater than marginal cost (MC), so the monopoly can make super-profits. Hence, for high outputs – when MC ≥ MR – the firm loses money.

- Being in control of the entire market, collusion and unjust monopolistic concentration of power among supposed competitors occur. Monopolistic firms like Credit Card firms, Banks, Cereal companies et cetera, can cause damage to both consumers and entrepreneurs because this development hinders and prevents the proper functioning and operation of markets. It constrains competition and innovation and also distorts true prices, thus punishing consumers who are overcharged (i.e. made to pay higher prices). This is considered harmful to the public interest.

Question 12

(a) Why are monopolies considered to be against the public interest? Discuss some of the measures that can be taken to regulate the activities of monopolies.

MODEL ANSWER:

Monopolies are usually criticized on the grounds that they cause a misallocation of resources by restricting the entry of new firms into the industry and charging prices that are above the marginal costs of production. The case against monopoly is usually made by comparison with a firm that is operating under conditions of perfect competition.

It is argued that under perfect competition the firm equates price to marginal costs and that the consumer pays for the satisfaction or utility he gains from consuming the marginal unit. Likewise, for the producer under perfect competition the marginal revenue of a unit of output equals the marginal cost of producing that output.

Figure 4.M

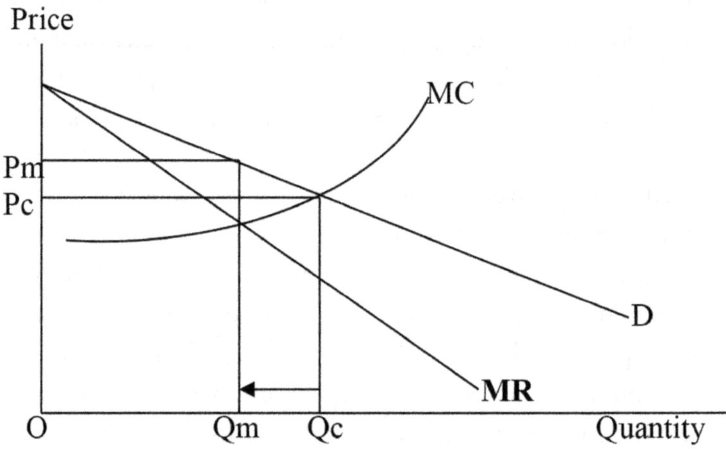

Figure 4.M illustrates these arguments. The demand curve facing the *monopolist* is labeled D. The curve labeled MC is the sum of the marginal costs of all firms in the industry; it is also the supply curve. The competitive price and output levels are given as PC and QC respectively. Now, let us assume that the industry is monopolized and that monopolization has no effect on the firms' cost curves. The competitive industry's supply curve will now become the monopolist's MC curve. A profit maximizing monopolist will now sell quantity QM charging price PM. Note that quantity QM is smaller than QC, and, given the demand curve confronting the firm, this implies *a higher price* after monopolization.

Another argument that is advanced against monopolies is that they have *no incentive to produce efficiently.* They are assured of their market and hence do not have the incentive to produce goods at minimum cost. The *quality of their products* will also tend to be lower, given the absence of competition and the presence of a secure market for the product. Against this, note that if a monopolist succeeds in reducing his costs his profits increase. Thus, he may have the same incentive to reduce costs as a firm under perfect competition.

If a monopoly is considered harmful to the public interest there is a number of measures that the government can take to deal with the problem. The government can:

- *Nationalize the monopoly* and operate it in the public interest. In this way, the public will be protected because the government can ensure that consumers are charged a realistic price. Should surplus profits be made, the government can pass these on to consumers in the form of lower prices or reduced taxation.

- Charge *lump sum tax* on the monopolist's output. Such a tax would be a fixed charge and would have no effect on the monopolist's price and output.

- Impose a *price ceiling* on the monopolist's sales. The effect of this measure would be to lower price and increase output.

Question 13

(a) Using suitable examples define barriers to entry. Explain how barriers to entry affect a firm's profits.

MODEL ANSWER:

Barriers to entry are defined as any impediments designed to prevent the entry of new firms into the industry. Factors which make it hard for new firms to **enter** an industry lead to fewer firms with limited pressure to compete (thereby limiting or preventing competition). Entry barriers are usually divided into *natural barriers* and *firm-created barriers.*

A. Natural barriers can take the form of:

* *Ownership of raw materials:* a firm that controls a natural resource input that is essential to the production of some final commodity can prevent rival firms from entering that industry by denying them access to sources of supply of that natural resource.

* *Indivisibilities:* the efficient scale of operation for a plant may be so large there is room for only one firm. Good examples are to be found in many public utility enterprises such as water, electricity, telephones and power generation. Such industries usually enjoy substantial economies of scale and at the same time competition in these industries would be impractical because unit costs for individual firms would be high. These costs act as an impediment to the entry of new firms into the industry. If you take for example the software industry (for a while dominated by Microsoft) or the commercial aircraft industry, the high cost of designing and testing and the initial investments for these industries are too high to permit ease of entry.

* *Government Policy:* in some industries government policy may prevent competition. The government may establish a single buyer/seller agency responsible for marketing all the output of that industry. Examples in Zimbabwe are the Mineral Marketing Corporation (MMZ), the Grain Marketing Board (GMB) and the Dairy Marketing Board (DMB). You have similar restrictions in Zambia like the Food Reserve Agency (FRA). The government may also issue patents and licenses to firms. Such patents prevent rival firms from entering that industry, at least for the duration of the patent or franchise.

Through legal restrictions, inventors are granted patents so that they can enjoy monopoly power which acts as an incentive for more research. Government may also impose entry restrictions for public utilities like water, telephones or electricity distribution. These measures create franchise monopolies, granting to the entrepreneur the exclusive right to produce or supply a service. Tariffs and quotas may also restrict units or competition, which could also lead to higher prices and costs.

B. Firm-created barriers to entry are:

* *Advertising:* If advertising creates lasting preferences for the products or service, this will act as a barrier to the entry of new firms. Because advertising can create product awareness and loyalty to well-known

brands, this can act a barrier to entry. For famous brands like Pepsi and Coca-Cola, adverts make it expensive for potential rivals.

* For such barriers to be effective there has to be economies of scale in advertising such that larger and more established firms are able to benefit from large discounts for their frequent extensive advertising. This would impose heavy costs on new entrants and prevent them from entering the industry. **Figure 4.13** below shows the relationship between advertising and costs. It shows that at higher output levels, costs of advertising per unit are lower.

* *Product differentiation*: this can increase the market power of the producers because a vast array of different brands, models or products are produced by few firms to satisfy a range of consumers. This discourages other potential competitors. Examples for this are cereal, auto, or cigarette companies. Recall that market structure depends on relative cost and demand factors. Thus, an oligopoly structure emerges when product differentiation constitutes an important feature of the market. This is because costs turn up at a higher level of output relative to the total industry demand-curve. In such a scenario, the coexistence of many perfectly competitive firms becomes impossible.

Figure 4.13

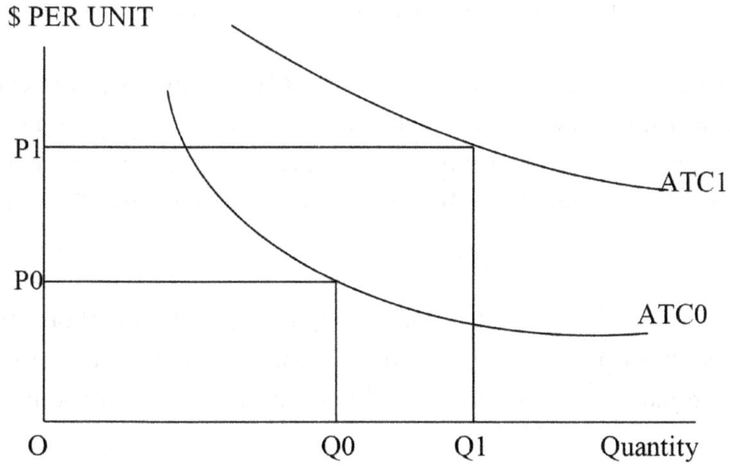

$ PER UNIT
P1
P0
ATC1
ATC0
O
Q0
Q1
Quantity

- *Brand proliferation:* many products can be differentiated considerably. If a firm has a large number of differentiated products, this can confer an advantage on that firm relative to other firms with fewer brands. Brand proliferation may be used as a pre-emptive strategy. The established firm can produce a wide range of products including those that a potential new entrant might be expected to produce.

- *Capital market imperfections:* different rates of interest may increase with the amount borrowed. Thus firms wishing to enter a particular industry may be confronted with different costs of capital relative to those facing larger established firms.

- *Consumer lock-in* and *switching costs:* may prevent consumers migrating to other firms. Just as *Network Externalities* in the telecommunications industry, for instance, could make entry difficult.

- *Predatory pricing:* to prevent other firms from entering the industry, a firm might offer its products at prices below the minimum average costs of production. The idea is to keep prices at that low level until the new entrant goes bankrupt.

- *Pre-emptive expansion:* firms may build new plants long before they are expected to operate at a profit. If so, it will not pay a new firm to risk building a new plant knowing that established firms will remain in possession of the market when demand eventually expands.

The existence of barriers to entry means that firms can charge prices that exceed minimum average costs of production and earn above normal profits, even in the long run. Entry barriers are usually associated with monopoly firms though they can also be found in oligopolistic markets.

Figure 4.14 shows how *entry barriers* help to create abnormal profits for a monopoly firm. When the monopolist charges a price P that exceeds the marginal cost of production, this enables him to earn abnormal profits. The abnormal profits earned are indicated by the shaded area in the diagram.

Figure 4.14

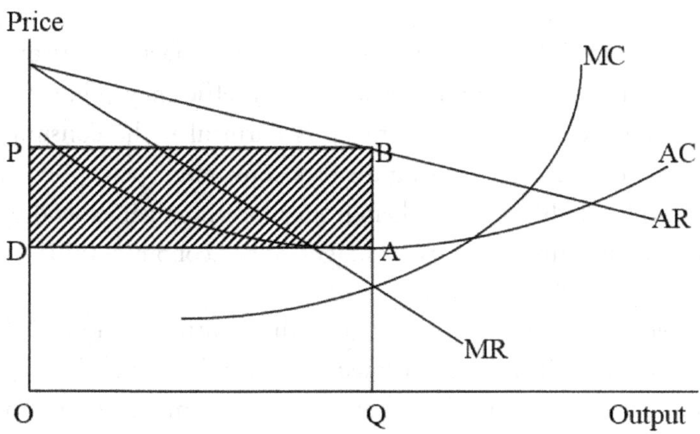

Question 14

(a) *In what ways might advertising by firms be:*
  (i) beneficial,
  (ii) harmful to the consumer's interests?

MODEL ANSWER:
There are two main types of advertising, namely *informative* and *persuasive.*

* *Informative advertising* aims to improve the consumer's knowledge of a product or service. This type of advertising can be explained by the fact that it is expensive for consumers to obtain information about products and many will always be ignorant about some products to some degree.

* *Persuasive advertising* attempts to alter consumers' tastes and preferences about products. For instance, much of the advertising that appears on television is of the persuasive type.

This distinction between persuasive and informative advertising is important to our understanding of the effects of advertising on the consumer, as we shall see shortly.

Advertising, whether informative or persuasive, affects the firm's total operating costs and this can result in a loss in efficiency. Thus, from an efficiency point of view all advertising is harmful if the consumers do not benefit from it. If advertising distorts consumers' perceptions about different products, this prevents them from allocating their expenditures in a manner that maximizes utility, as suggested by economics utility theory.

Informative advertising, by improving the consumer's knowledge of products, can result in a more informed choice on the part of the consumer while persuasive advertising, by distorting the consumer's perceptions, can lead him to make the wrong consumption choices.

However, apart from improving the consumer's knowledge of different products, there are *several other ways in which advertising can benefit the consumer.*

- If advertising is successful, it should result in higher sales per unit of output and higher profits which the producer could then share with his consumers by charging lower prices for his products.

- Without advertising, it would be difficult for firms to introduce new products. Consumers would only know about the products after seeing them in the shops. Advertising, by informing consumers of the range of products available and the merits and demerits of these products, enables consumers to make more informed choices.

- Looking at the economy as a whole, it can be argued that advertising helps to keep the level of employment high. If it is successful, sales for goods and services will be high and more jobs will be generated to meet the extra demand. By the same token, this will help to keep business confidence high.

Question 15

(a) What is an oligopolistic market?

(i) Discuss some of its important features.

(ii) Explain how prices and output are determined in an oligopolistic market.

MODEL ANSWER:

(i) **Oligopoly** is a market dominated by a few, often large firms (suppliers), and is characterized by heavy ***product differentiation*** through: advertising, non-price competition, quality of service and other market ploys. This situation is different from an industry with too many small firms operating at less than optimal capacity, thereby creating excess capacity. Since oligopolists abhor price competition, *interdependence* makes them cautious about price wars.

Product prices of these firms tend to be sticky and are close to avoid triggering price competition. For instance, American fast food firms like Burger King, McDonalds and Wendy's keep their prices close to each other's. The News Media market provides another example.

Because these firms are *interdependent*, the behavior of each firm has an impact on the other firms. Conversely, the reaction and behavior of rival firms determine the behavior of their competitors. That is, assumptions are made about other firms' reactions. In this industry, *leadership pricing* is common.

To illustrate, if one firm (usually the leader) raises the price, others follow. But if others do not follow suit that firm risks losing market share. And, if one firm cuts the price, others are likely to cut theirs too. But since price wars lead to everyone losing money, the avoidance of price competition tends to be the norm. When a price leader, let's say a Gas Station, announces its new price per liter, it waits for others *to react.* A similar reaction happens when one Bank announces a change in prime interest-rate, others follow suit.

MODEL ANSWER:

(ii) Given that in **oligopoly,** that is, a market where there are a few firms who compete within a given industry, it is very important for each firm to know what its ***rivals*** are doing, the behavior of participants in the market tends to be interdependent. This *interdependence* means that each firm must pay close attention to the likely *reaction* of its rivals when planning its marketing strategy. The independence of firms under oligopoly is very useful for analyzing their behavior as the example below illustrates.

Note, that in perfect competition or in a monopolistic structure, there are, respectively, many firms or one firm that does not have to consider the actions of others. In developed market economies practical oligopoly examples can be found in: the News Media, Soft Drinks, Beer and Airline Industries. In the airline industry for example, one airline – usually a *price leader*, changes the price to modify demand in the market. If this firm increases fares, it waits for rivals to *react* or *match* it. Depending on others' reaction, it may or may not adjust the price in response. For fear of losing market share, it certainly backs off if rivals refuse to follow suit.

In theory this is how it works. Imagine a market situation which is comprised of two firms A and B who manufacture a given product at ***a price*** (cost) of $1 per unit output. If both firms set a (selling) price of $5 per unit, each firm will sell 100 units and make a profit of $4 per unit or $400 per month. If both firms set their price at $4 per unit, each firm can sell 120 units and make a profit of $360 per month. Given these assumptions, what prices will each firm charge?

Clearly, a price of $5 per unit would maximize their joint profits but under oligopoly this will not represent a stable market situation. **Table 4.3** below represents the alternative pricing strategies as they appear to company A.

If A cuts his price while B keeps his price constant, A will attract many of B's customers. On the other hand, if B cuts his price while A's price remains constant at $5, B will attract many of A's customers leaving A with only $240 in profit. Thus, to set his price, A needs to make an assumption about how B is going *to react* to any moves that he may make.

Table 4.3

		B's Pricing Strategy	
		$ 5	$4
A's Pricing Strategy	$5	$400	$240
	$4	$450	$360

Question 15

(b) *Given this interdependence in oligopoly, how will the two firms determine their price and output levels?*

MODEL ANSWER:

Let us look at some of the possibilities:

* Firms in an oligopoly recognize that it is almost futile to compete on the basis of price. Thus they will tacitly coordinate their actions with those of their rivals. Each firm will imitate the price and output strategies of other firms and seek to maximize *joint profits*. In other words, they try to anticipate the actions of their rivals and act in ways that avoid harming the overall interests of participating firms.

* Firms may work under the assumption that their rivals will do the worst. For example, firm A may operate on the assumption that firm

B will cut its price and may therefore decide to cut his price first. If every firm in the industry follows the same reasoning they will all end up reducing their prices.

* Each firm will expect its rivals to match its price decreases but not its price increases. Under this assumption, a firm will be reluctant to lower its prices because it realizes that this might provoke a price war with each firm trying to beat the other firm's price reductions.

The *interdependence* of firms under oligopoly is usually illustrated by means of a *kinked demand* diagram as shown in **Figure 4.15**. This diagram is based on the assumption that if a firm cuts it price other firms will match the price decrease and therefore the firm will not lose its market share.

Figure 4.15

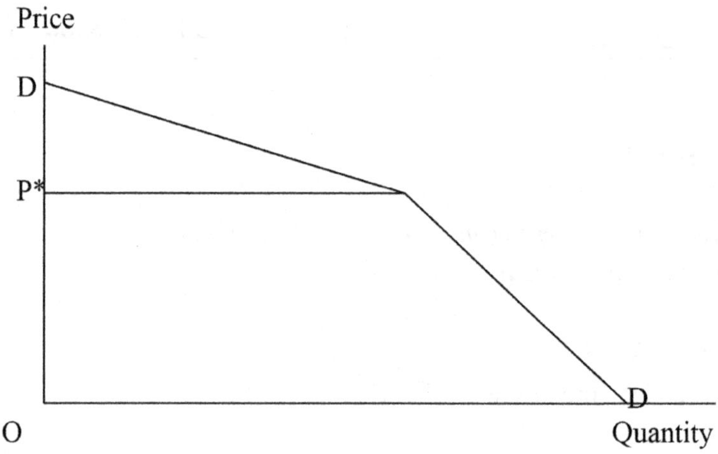

In the diagram **(Fig 4.15)** assume that P* is the market price. Assume further that the firm reduces its price below P*. Other firms will respond by making similar price cuts and sales in the industry as a whole will expand. The price cutting firm will thus fail to expand its market share; it will simply sell more at a lower price. In contrast, if the firm increases its price other firms in the industry may not follow its move and the firm will lose its market share. In the case of a price decrease, demand will be inelastic and in the case of a price increase demand will be elastic.

While this theory is simple and elegant it has one major weakness. It does not explain how prices come to be determined in the first place.

The different explanations suggest that prices are likely to be unstable under an oligopoly. For this reason, firms under oligopoly will tend to favour *non-price forms* of competition such as advertising, after sales service, and other strategies.

Question 15

(c) Can you explain how the oligopoly model can be used to limit competition from rivals? By –
(i) Strategic entry deterrence
(ii) Predatory pricing

MODEL ANSWER:

(i) Strategic entry deterrence – is a strategy to prevent other firms from entering the market through, for example, **limit pricing**, which is charging a price lower than the profit maximizing price in order to keep other firms out. When an established firm sets a price below the profit maximizing one, the new entrant would *not find it profitable* to enter at that lower price. But yet the established firm, especially over time, can still make *positive profit* or at least *zero economic profit.*

(ii) Predatory pricing – Is a strategy of lowering prices below marginal cost (MC) to drive rival firms out of the industry and scare off potential entrants. This is not common, however, because when a firm lowers its price below cost, it incurs losses, which it hopes to recoup through future profits.

The predator must also convince other firms that it will keep its price low until rivals leave the market. If, after they leave, the predator raises the price that in turn may attract new entrants. In which case, the cycle is repeated.

But if all firms have equal costs (i.e. they are facing the same MC), the predator risks incurring larger losses than rivals. Although recouping losses from future profits is difficult, aggressive predatory tactics might indeed scare away other firms and deter new entrants, thereby achieving the firm's ultimate objective.

Question 15

(d) Clearly demonstrate that you understand the theory behind Kinked Demand Curve.

MODEL ANSWER:

Kinked-demand curve is a *non-cooperative oligopoly* model. It is assumed that a firm is faced with two demand curves: the *first one* (D1) reflects the demand for its products IF all rival firms follow a given price change; the *second one* (D2) is for demand IF rivals do not follow price change. Demand curve one (D1) is more elastic than demand curve two (D2). Where the two cross forms a kink.(see **Figure 4.16**).

Figure 4.16

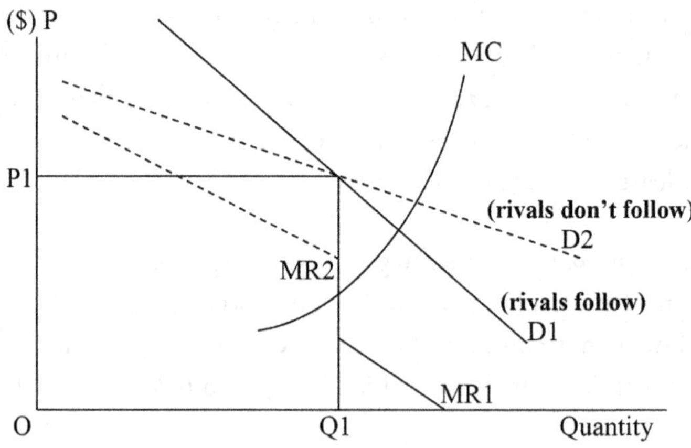

Kinked-Demand Curve Model

Question 15

(e) What are the two common oligopolistic models?

MODEL ANSWER:

Basically there are two different types of oligopolistic models: (1) the *non-cooperative* one and (2) the *cooperative oligopoly.*

(i) The *non-cooperative* one, depicted by the **Kinked Demand** curve, means that managers make decisions based on a strategy that anticipates the behavior of rivals. By assuming that rivals want to inflict maximum damage on their competitors, managers take precautions to respond to this challenge. However, their ultimate aim is: to cooperate or coordinate their actions with other rivals.

(ii) In a *cooperative oligopoly*, the assumption is that firms explicitly or implicitly cooperate with each other to achieve outcomes beneficial to all. The fear is that if firms do not collabourate or coordinate their actions, both (or all) would be worse off. But because in this model there are incentives for cheating on cooperative behavior, there is a necessity for regulations to minimize any illegal behavior.

Cartels - represent good examples of cooperative oligopoly: OPEC for crude oil and the DIAMOND Cartel led by South Africa being specific examples. In this model, firms (or countries) agree to coordinate their behavior regarding pricing and output decisions for the sake of maximizing profits. As observed, since Cartel members may also have an incentive to cheat on cartel agreements, it is sometimes difficult to maintain cartel behavior.

OPEC was founded in the 1970s to counter the market power of major oil companies, at a time when the demand for crude oil was high. As prices hiked, this caused severe shocks. Saudi Arabia, the largest oil supplier with cost advantage, accumulated market power which she would use sometimes to control the behavior of other Cartel members.

In the case of the DIAMOND Cartel – De Beers (owned by the Oppenheimer family) controls production. This cartel uses an explicit set of rules aimed at *controlling supply* so as to maintain **scarcity** and the **perceived value** of diamonds. By strategically preventing other diamond mining firms from entry, De Beers then basically remains the dominant presence in the field as a "*single firm*". The result is that this *Diamond Syndicate* also controls prices.

Because of bloody wars in some African countries and conflicts in diamond supply countries like Democratic Republic of Congo (DRC) and Sierra Leone, a process known as: the **Kimberly Process**, under the auspices of UN, was introduced to certify the source of diamonds. However, due to lack of cooperation with other firms (or countries) outside the Diamond Syndicate and by circumventing UN organs, De Beers' strict control on diamonds continues.

Not all *cooperative oligopolies* are useful because they can engage in "**tacit collusion**" behavior. For this reason, in some countries like the USA and others in the European Union (EU) *anti-trust laws* exist to discourage illegal cartels or any firms from engaging in tacit collusion – coordinated behavior attained without formal agreement. Examples of tacit cooperation include: collusion to set *uniform prices* among perceived rivals or *Swaps and Exchanges* of goods between colluding firms. The latter is made possible when a firm in one location sells output to local customers of another firm in another location in return for a rendered service to the rival firm.

Question 15

(f) Explain how game theory is a type of non-cooperative oligopoly model.

MODEL ANSWER:

Game theory represents *non-cooperative oligopolistic behavior* in the market place. Such behavior results from the fact that prices, product supplies and profits are all functions of *strategic behavior* on the part of interdependent rival firms in the market. The **Prisoners' Dilemma** model is a dominant strategy type which results in the *best outcome* or highest payoff accruing to a given player (firm) no matter what action or choice the other player (firm) makes.

Imagine you have two prisoners caught by Police after committing a crime and are interrogated in two separate prison cells. An offer of exemption from incarceration is made to them separately: if he/she confesses, he/she gets no prison (0 years) but the information obtained from him/her would be used to send the friend to prison for fifteen (15) years. The responses of the two prisoners are illustrated in **Table 4.4** below.

Table 4.4

		PRISONER PHIRI	
		Don't Confess	**Confess**
PRISONER MWAMBA	**Don't Confess**	3yrs, 3yrs	15yrs, 0yrs
	Confess	0yrs, 15yrs	7yrs, 7yrs

Note from the table that: If both were to confess, each would get seven (7) years. But if neither confessed, they would only get each three (3) years. But being in separate cells and unable to communicate, they are unaware of each other's choices. So with coordination and their willingness to trust each other, the *best choice* possible could have been attained. This is a choice which could only come out of a cooperative model of oligopoly. Being unable to cooperate or reach an agreement is the *dilemma* some oligopoly firms face. Hence, the term non-cooperative behavior. And since the Prisoners' Dilemma is a dominant strategy, both tend to confess with each ending up with seven (7) years in prison. But in repeat actions or decisions, such as those taken by firms, learning from the past occurs thereby reducing pain from bad choices or cheating.

5 National Income Determination and Theory of Distribution

Question 1

(a) Define and explain the concepts of average propensity to save and the marginal propensity to save.

MODEL ANSWER:

The *average propensity to save* (APS) describes the proportion of *total disposable income* that is not consumed. It is measured using the formula:

$$APS = \frac{S}{Yd}$$

Where: S is the level of saving and Yd is the total level of disposable income. Alternatively, the APS can be measured using the formula:

$$APS = 1 - \frac{C}{Yd}$$

Where: C is consumption; and Yd is total disposable income.

The *marginal propensity to save*, MPS, tells us how much of a given increase in income will be saved. It is measured using the following formula:

$$MPS = \frac{\text{Change in saving}}{\text{Change in income}}$$

This relationship is illustrated in **Figure 5.1**. The line labeled S denotes the *saving function* and ΔS and ΔY denote *marginal changes* in the levels of savings and income respectively.

Figure 5.1

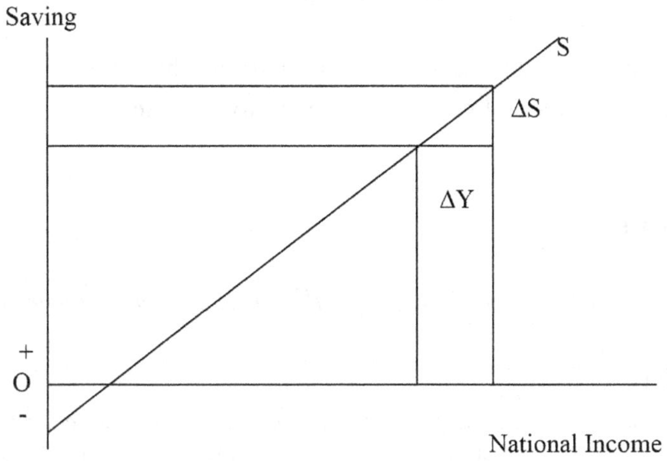

Saving

S

ΔS

ΔY

+
O
-

National Income

Question 1

(b) Analyze the economic effects of:
(i) an increase in the level of saving,
(ii) a decrease in the level of saving.

MODEL ANSWER:

(i) *Saving* is defined as income that is *not consumed* and as such represents a leakage from the circular flow of income. Another way of saying this is that, saving is that part of income that is paid out by households but is not returned to them through the spending of households. If national income is in equilibrium and the level of injections equals leakages, *an increase* in the level of saving will result in some firm's output remaining unsold. If this happens, firms will respond by reducing production so that output and employment will fall. Equilibrium national income will be restored when the level of injections equals leakages.

(ii) A *reduction* in the level of saving will have the opposite effect to that outlined above, starting from a position in which national income is in equilibrium, if the level of *savings decreases.*

Injections will exceed leakages at the original equilibrium point. To restore equilibrium, the level of nation income has to increase.

Question 2

(a) Define national income and explain the problems involved in measuring it.

MODEL ANSWER:

National income is a measure of the *total flow of output* in an economy over a given time period which is usually one year. The main problems involved in measuring national income are as follows.

* Valuation: The prices of goods and services are used as a measure of their value. However, problems arise when the level of prices changes as often happens in practice. Such price changes make it difficult to compare price changes from year to year. A related problem is that the national income accountant must assume that relative prices of goods and services are a reasonable reflection of the satisfaction to be gained from the consumption of different commodities. For example, if a pack of cigarettes costs twice as much as a pint of beer, the accountant must assume that a pint of beer gives twice as much satisfaction as a pack of cigarettes. In reality, however, this assumption may not be correct.

* Public goods: Some goods and services do not have market prices. Many public services such as defense, law and order, health, bridges and education fall into this category. However, since such services *satisfy human wants* they are regarded as production and should be included in the national income accounts. In practice, such services are usually *valued at cost,* that is, the cost of providing them is taken

as a measure of their value. For example, a teacher's salary would be taken as a measure of this contribution to total output.

* Self-provided goods: These give rise to additional problems. For example, in many developing country communities farmers consume most of their output of goods and services. Where similar goods and services are sold on the market, it may be possible to give self-provided goods an estimated valuation based on the prices paid for similar goods and services.

* Double counting: Adding up the total of all firms in the country will result in double counting. Part of the value of any firm's output consists of raw material inputs of other components at an earlier stage of the production process. Thus, only the value added at each stage should be included in the final accounts.

* Taxes and subsidies: Finally, market prices may be distorted by taxes and subsidies. If so, they will not reflect the true costs of production. To arrive at factor cost valuation, it is necessary to deduct all taxes and add all subsidies.

Question 3

(a) What are the main components of Aggregate Monetary Demand (AMD) in Zimbabwe/Zambia?

MODEL ANSWER:

The main components of aggregate monetary demand in Zimbabwe or Zambia are consumption (C), Investment (I), Government Expenditure (G), minus Savings (S), Imports (I), and taxes (T). These can be further classified into *injections* (C+I+G) and *leakages* (S+T+M). These components are described in more detail below.

* Consumption: Total consumption by *households* is one of the main components of aggregate money demand (AMD) in many countries, including Zimbabwe or Zambia. Included under this heading are

purchases of all durable goods such as clothing items and expenditure on services such as haircuts, restaurant meals and education.

* Saving: Saving is defined as *income that is not consumed.* In other words, if Y is total income then we have that:

$$Y = C + S$$

where C = total consumption;
S = saving;
and Y= income
therefore Y= C + S
or, Y-S = C

Question 3

(b) What are the possible economic consequences of a change in one of the components described above?

MODEL ANSWER:
To analyze the effect of a change in *government expenditure* (G) it is necessary to define the concept of equilibrium income. This is the level of income achieved when total *injections* equal total *leakages.* Another factor that has a bearing on this analysis is that:

- An increase in injections will increase national income, a decrease will reduce it.

- An increase in leakages will reduce national income, a decrease will raise it.

Other things being equal, if national income is in equilibrium and the *government expenditure increases*, this will have the effect of disturbing the initial equilibrium and injections will exceed leakages.

National income will increase and leakages, which are a function of national income, will also increase until equilibrium is re-established at the higher level of national income. A *fall in government expenditure* has the opposite effect. Because government expenditure is an injection, a reduction in government expenditure will cause national income to fall. Leakages which are also a function of national income will also fall until equilibrium is re-established at a lower level of national income.

Figure 5.2 helps to clarify the analysis. Y^1 is the initial equilibrium and the curves labeled C+I+G represent different levels of aggregate demand. If government spending increases the aggregate expenditure line shifts horizontally upwards from $C+I+G^1$ to $C+I+G^2$ and national income increases, to a new equilibrium at Y^2. Conversely, a fall in government expenditure from the initial equilibrium pushes the aggregate demand curve horizontally downwards from $C+I+G^1$ to $C+G+I^3$ and income falls to new equilibrium Y^3.

Figure 5.2

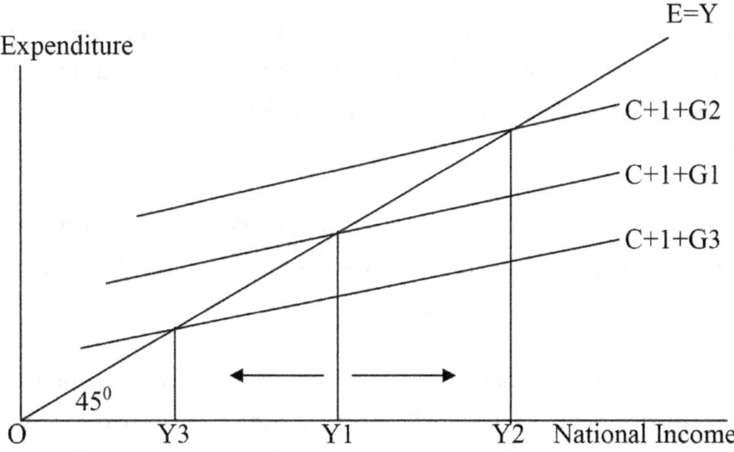

Question 4

(a) *To what extent are international comparisons of GNP satisfactory indicators of relative living standards in different countries?*

MODEL ANSWER:

The standard of living of different countries can be compared by referring to statistics in order to *compare living standards* of different countries but this methodology is fraught with problems.

Apart from the problem of defining “the standard of living” great care is needed when using statistics for international comparisons. The fact that one country has a higher per capita income than another does not necessarily mean that the standard of living of its inhabitants is higher.

The standard of living of a country depends on many factors such as the type of goods consumed by the community as well as the *social and economic environment* offered in that country. Per capita Gross National Product (GNP) measures do not reflect these factors some of which are extremely difficult to quantify. Neither do they reveal the relative burden of taxation in different countries nor the social welfare facilities that are provided by the government. Furthermore, within a given country, large variations in regional incomes may exist, which are not revealed in the statistics.

An important consideration is that *per capita income* is often measured in gross figures. However, this may itself be misleading if the levels of depreciation differ between countries.

Another problem is that there may be different rates of inflation prevailing in the countries being considered, types of goods consumed etc. When differences in inflation exist, adjustments need to be made to take account of the differences in purchasing power.

The rate of exchange of national currencies may not be a good indicator of the relative purchasing power of different currencies. For example, if one Zimbabwe dollar exchanges for two Zambian kwacha it does not follow that $1 in Zimbabwe will buy as much as K2 in Zambia. The exchange rate in a particular country usually reflects the *economic policies* being pursued by that country and only takes into account the prices of goods that enter into international trade.

By definition, per capita GNP is an average measure and as such tends to disguise wide extremes in the distribution of income. Two countries may have the same income per head but if income is more evenly distributed in one country than another then the standards of living will differ.

We also need to consider the composition of goods that are produced for consumption. For example a country may spend more on defense. Such expenditure would appear in the statistics in the same way as consumption or capital expenditure. However, other things being equal if one country spends less on defense than another country, it in fact enjoys a higher standard of living.

Furthermore, GNP figures do not reveal the range of goods available for consumption nor the quality of education or standards of literacy.

Some of the differences in standards of living arise due to climate and geography. In cold climates people spend a relatively large proportion of their income on keeping warm while in sparsely populated countries people may need to spend more on transport.

The accuracy of GNP statistics and the proportion of goods exchanged for money may differ widely between countries. In developing countries such as Zimbabwe or Zambia, the compilation of accurate statistics is difficult and the final figures usually involve some element of guesswork. Moreover, in many developing countries much of the output is consumed by the producer and does not enter into the GNP statistics.

For these reasons, a *meaningful comparison* of the standard of living between counties should not be based on GNP figures alone. It needs to be supplemented by other social indicators such as pupil/teacher ratio, number of doctors per head of the population, number of hospital beds, urban congestion, pollution and so forth.

Question 5

(a) Distinguish between transfer earnings and economic rent. Use examples in your answer.

MODEL ANSWER:

Transfer earnings are defined as the minimum amount that must be earned to prevent a factor of production from transferring to another use. *Economic rent* is said to be earned whenever a factor of production receives a reward that exceeds its transfer earnings. The concepts of transfer earnings and economic rent apply to all factors of production that are **fixed** in supply, such as land. Thus, doctors, sportsmen and film stars are in relatively fixed supply and hence, a large portion of their high earnings represent economic rent.

When the demand for fixed land increases, such as spiked by population increase, the price tends to rise.

The distinction between *transfer earnings* and *economic rent* is best illustrated by means of an example. To determine the transfer earnings of, say, a teacher, we need to ask what the teacher would earn in his next best occupation. Let us say that if he were to leave teaching his next best occupation would be painting and that this would pay him $300 per month. The $300 is his transfer earnings. Furthermore, suppose that a teacher's salary is 400 per month. Then his economic rent is $400-$300=$100.

The earnings of most factors of production consist of economic rent and transfer earnings; there are two exceptions, however. These occur:

- When the supply curve is perfectly inelastic and all earnings become economic rent.
- When the supply curve is perfectly elastic and all earnings become transfer earnings.

The concepts of transfer earnings and economic rent are illustrated in **Figure 5.3.**

Figure 5.3

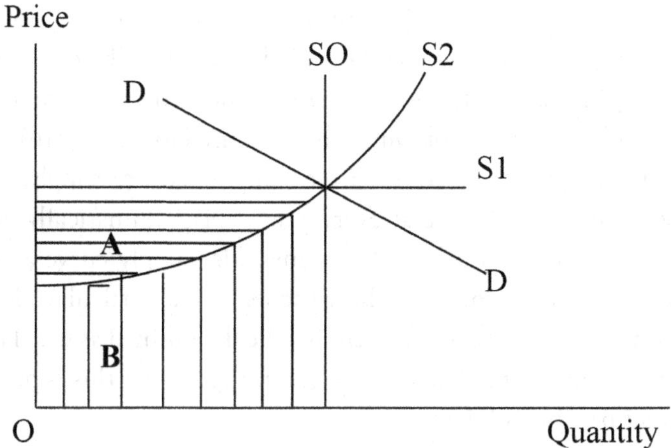

A = Economic rent
B = Transfer earnings

With supply curve S2 transfer earnings are B and economic rent is A. With supply curve S1 all earnings are transfer earnings. With supply curve SO all earnings are economic rent.

Question 5

(b) What is quasi-rent?

MODEL ANSWER:
In the *short run* certain factors of production are fixed in supply. In the long run, it may be possible to increase the supply of the factor in which case the rent element will disappear. The rent element that accrues to the factor in the short run is known as *quasi-rent.*

Question 5

(c) *With the aid of a diagram illustrate how the rent for a particular piece of land is determined.*

MODEL ANSWER:

The total quantity of *land is fixed* in supply: unlike the other factors of production such as capital and labour the available supply of land cannot be readily or easily increased. However human ingenuity displayed for ex., by the Chinese and the Emiratis of Dubai; is being used to create artificial islands. But restricting our focus for the time being to nature's supply, the total quantity of land is the same at every price. Diagrammatically, we show this by means of a vertical (perfectly inelastic) supply curve as in **Figure 5.4**. The same diagram shows how the *rent* for a particular piece of land is determined. The free market rent will be determined as usual by intersection of the supply and demand curves. In **Figure 5.4** this is point E, where the rent payable is R1.

Figure 5.4

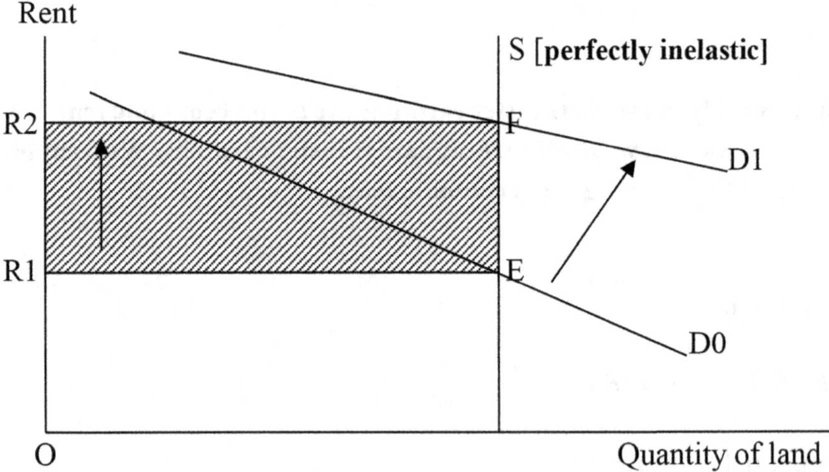

Suppose that as a result of an increase in population in Harare or Lusaka the demand for land increases (e.g., as a result of population increase), so, the demand curve will shift from D0 to D1 in Figure 5.4 and the rent will increase to R2 at point F.

The above analysis explains why *rent levels* are usually high in city centre sites. The reason for this is that the *demand for land* in these areas is higher than in the outskirts of the city, so rents there will also be higher.

If the demand for land increases, we would expect this to have two effects on the utilization of land:

- It will be profitable to employ land that was formerly unprofitable.
- People will utilize the available land more effectively, for example, by building multi-story buildings instead of single or double-story.

Question 6

(a) Define profit. Use suitable examples in your answer.

MODEL ANSWER:

Profit is defined as the **reward for risk-taking** or the **reward for uncertainty bearing**. An entrepreneur who goes into business faces many risks. For example, there is the risk of damage to his premises because they may catch fire; or, there is the risk of theft. Of all the risks that the entrepreneur faces, there are some that can be *insured against* and thus pose no serious problem for the entrepreneur. However, there are other risks that cannot be insured against. For example, a firm cannot insure against the possibility of changes in demand or cost conditions for its product. To be precise, therefore, we should define profits as the reward for *non-insurable risks.*

Question 6

(b) How does profit differ from the earnings of other factors of production?

MODEL ANSWER:

Profit differs from the earnings of other factors of production in a number of ways. These are:

- Profit can be negative whereas the earnings to other factors of production are generally positive.

- In general, profit levels fluctuate more than the earnings to other factors of production.

- While wages, interest and rent are contractual in nature and fairly certain to be earned, profit is a residue and is subject to more uncertainty.

Question 6

(c) Describe the functions of profit in a free market.

MODEL ANSWER:

In a free market profit performs several functions:

- It acts as an inducement for firms to *accept the risks of going into business*. Risk is inherent in any business undertaking and profit is necessary to encourage entrepreneurs to go into business despite these risks.

- It is an important source of funds for investment. *Retained profits* can be ploughed back into the business which is a cheaper way of raising capital than borrowing from sources external to the firm.

- It *encourages innovation*. It is the expectation of high profits that encourages firms to innovate. Innovation in turn stimulates investment, total employment and output.

- It ensures that production is undertaken by the *most efficient* firms. Firms whose profits are rising will be experiencing falling costs of production while those with falling profits will be experiencing higher costs and may eventually be driven out of business.

Question 7

(a) What is the Marginal Productivity Theory of Wages? Illustrate your answer with a diagram.

MODEL ANSWER:

The Marginal Productivity Theory of Wages is concerned with analyzing the **conditions** that determine the demand for labour under conditions of perfect competition. It shows that under such conditions an entrepreneur will always pay a wage equal to the full value of the contribution of that unit of labour to total production.

To illustrate the principle we need to know the factors that determine demand for labour. The demand for labour is made not for its own sake but for what it contributes to total output (that is, its marginal physical product or MPP for short). The price that an entrepreneur pays for each unit of labour will depend on the addition to total receipts which results from the employment of that unit. This is known as the marginal revenue product (MRP) and equals the MPP *x* price of the product.

Diagrammatically the theory is illustrated in **Figure 5.5**. The diagram shows that the entrepreneur will pay a wage equal to OW and employ OM units of labour.

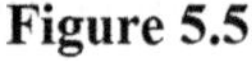

Figure 5.5

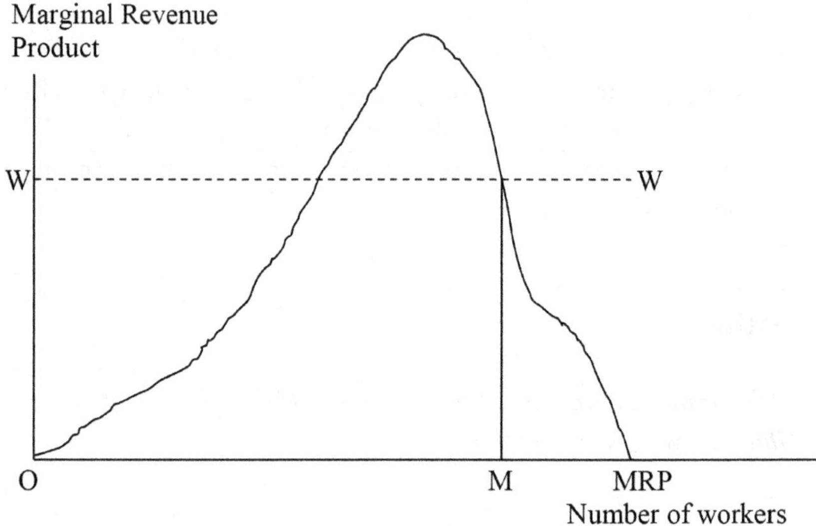

Question 7

(b) How useful is this marginal productivity theory as an explanation of wage levels?

MODEL ANSWER:

The *weakness of the theory* as an explanation of wage levels is as follows:

- It is too theoretical. It assumes perfect competition but in the real world conditions of perfect competition do not prevail.

- The productivity of labour often depends on the efficiency of co-operating factors such as capital and is not confined to the merits of labour alone. If so, it becomes difficult to separate the influence of the co-operating factors on total output.

* Oftentimes, theoretical assumptions do not match real world situations.

* It is not easily evaluated for certain classes of labour such as policemen, teachers, nurses, financial planners, dance instructors and others who are employed in the *service sector*. It is virtually impossible to measure their MPP as there is no physical product resulting from their work.

* Finally, empirical evidence indicates that expectations of profitability influence employers' hiring decisions far more than the level of wages.

* Despite these problems, the *marginal productivity theory* of wages is a useful description of the conditions underlying the demand for labour.

Question 8

(a) Describe some of the ways in which a trade union can secure a wage increase for its members.

MODEL ANSWER:

There are three main ways in which a trade union can secure a **wage increase** for its members.

* *By restricting the supply of labour:* Strong trade unions are usually able to restrict the supply of labour in their occupations. The effect of this is illustrated in **Figure 5.6**. Trade union action reduces the supply of labour from S-S1. As a result the wage rises from OW-OW1. There are a number of ways in which the supply of labour can be restricted. The union can insist on long apprenticeship periods designed to create shortages in a particular occupation. Another measure that is often applied is the closed shop agreement whereby only union members are eligible to apply for employment in that occupation. In some cases *strike action* is also used to demand minimum wages.

* *By fixing a minimum wage:* This method works well when the union is strong. If so, it can negotiate with employers for a minimum wage.

In Zimbabwe and Zambia, the government fixes the minimum wage through legislation and/or consultation with the Trade Unions.

* *By supporting measures to increase the demand for labour:* Where the union can influence the demand for labour this will have the effect of increasing the wage rate. The situation is illustrated in **Figure 5.6.** Initially, the marginal revenue product (MRP) curve (the firm's demand curve for labour) is given by MRP in the diagram; now assume that this shifts to MRP1. This will increase the wage rate from OW – OW1.

Figure 5.6

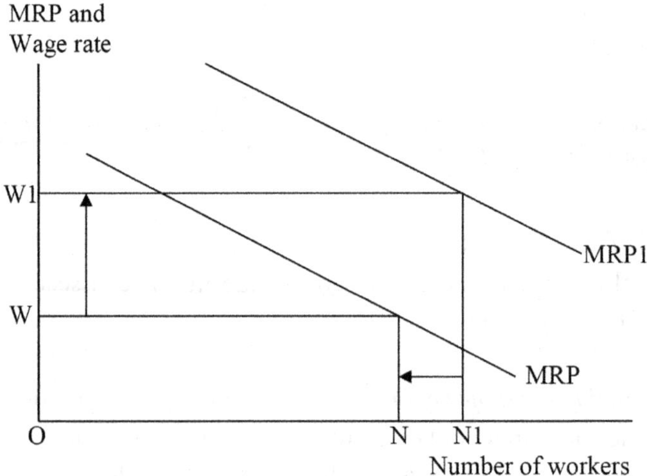

Question 8

(b) *What factors restrict the Trade Union's ability to secure wage increases? Use suitable diagrams in your answer.*

MODEL ANSWER:

The ability of the trade union to obtain a *wage increase* for its members will depend to some extent on whether conditions of *perfect competition prevail.* Under conditions of perfect competition, firms in the economy may be earning *abnormal profits* in the short run. Thus, trade unions are in a strong position to influence the level of wages in a strong economy and, in view of the abnormal profits, firms would find it difficult to refuse union demands for higher wages. In the long run, firms under perfect competition earn only *normal profits* and an increase in wages during those periods would cause unemployment. To see this, refer to **Figure 5.6** again.

Assume initially that ON1 people are employed earning wage rate W. The trade union demands wage rate OW1, which is granted. This will result in a fall in employment from ON1-ON. The size of the fall in employment ON-ON1 depends on the **elasticity of demand** for labour.

This in turn is influenced by the following factors:

* *Ease of substitution between different factors of production:* Where factors of production can be substituted with relative ease, demand for labour will tend to be inelastic. For example, an increase in wages will result in entrepreneurs substituting more capital for labour.

* *Elasticity of supply of other factors of production:* A rise in wages across industries will result in all firms demanding alternative factors of production. This will bid up the price of the factors. If so, the extent to which factors of production can be substituted will be limited.

* *Proportion of labour costs to total costs:* Where labour costs form a small proportion of total costs demand for labour is likely to be inelastic. The converse is also true.

* *Elasticity of demand for final product:* The demand for labour is *derived demand*; labour is not demanded for its own sake but for the goods that it produces. When demand for a commodity is elastic, a decrease in demand for it will reduce the demand for labour and cause a large fall in employment. The converse is also true.

Under conditions of imperfect competition firms may be earning abnormal profits and financially they are in a better position to grant their workers a wage increase. The success of the trade union in this case depends on many factors including the strength of the union, the amount of abnormal profits being earned and so forth.

Other general considerations are the level of employment in the economy, the cost of living and productivity. Where the level of productivity has increased the union is in a strong position to press for a wage increase while conditions of high unemployment such as those prevailing in Zimbabwe and Zambia particularly for youth generally work against trade unions' bargaining power. Finally, when the cost of living has gone up, unions may use this fact to press for higher wages.

Question 9

(a) Why is the distribution of income unequal?

MODEL ANSWER:

The distribution of income may be unequal for the following reasons:

* *Differences in natural ability:* People differ in their physical and mental abilities. Some individuals have the aptitude and intellectual capacity to enter professions such as medicine, law and accountancy and thus can command high earnings upon completion of their training. Others possess the talents needed to become musicians or artists while others have the physical stamina needed to become professional athletes. On the other end of the range, some individuals are forced to accept low paying jobs because they lack the natural talents and/or training needed to enter highly paid professions.

* *Education and training:* Human capital theory explains differences in income distribution by focusing on individual investments in education and training. Generally speaking, an individual's earnings will be related to the amount of education or training that he has

received. The higher the training or education, the higher the income. The amount of training a person receives is, in some cases, a matter of choice. Thus, one individual may choose to leave school early and obtain a job while another may opt to stay on in the education system. In other cases, however, individuals may lack the financial resources or ability needed to obtain education or training. The relationship between education and training and level of income is illustrated in **Figure 5.7** which is self-explanatory.

* *Job taste and willingness to take risks:* Some individuals may be willing to accept difficult or unpleasant tasks which require long hours of work and as a result they are likely to earn more. Also, occupations in which a high level of risk is involved often pay higher incomes than those which are relatively safe. Thus an entrepreneur who gambles successfully on the introduction of a new product can expect to earn high financial rewards. This is also illustrated by nurses willing to work in Emergency Rooms (ER) – they tend to have higher earnings per hour than those on normal shifts.

* *Property ownership:* The ownership of property and hence the receipt of property income in the form of rent, interest or profit is unevenly distributed in many countries. This results in substantial differences in income. Owners of property such as real estate earn good income.

* *Market power:* In the labour market powerful trade unions can often obtain wage increases for their members that are far above the average for their professions. Some occupations restrict entry to the occupation by insisting on long apprenticeship periods. As a result, earnings in these occupations are likely to be high because the supply of that particular skill is *restricted.* In the product market, a firm's profits and hence the incomes of those who work in it are likely to be high, if the firm can exercise some form of monopoly power. Doctors, engineers and lawyers are some of the restrictive professions which reward members handsomely.

* *Luck, connections and misfortune:* Finally, there are the non-economic factors such as luck, misfortune and good social or professional connections. A person may just be lucky in obtaining a well-paying job or he may benefit from being "at the right place at the right time" or because he knows the "right" people and has "right" connections. On the other hand, misfortunes such as the death of a family breadwinner and unemployment can result in relative poverty for the entire family.

Figure 5.7

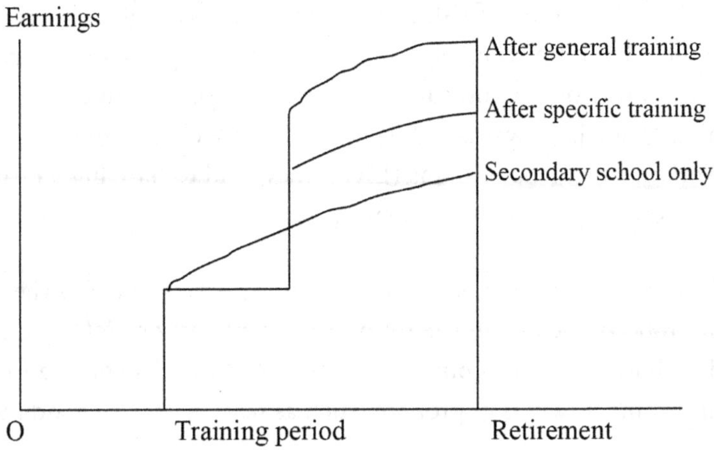

Question 10

(a) What is interest?

MODEL ANSWER:

Interest is the payment for the use of money. An interest rate of 10% means that the borrower pays 10% interest on every dollar that he borrows.

Question 10

(b) Explain why the banks charge interest on loans.

MODEL ANSWER:

There are three main reasons why banks charge interest on loans:

- to compensate for the risk that the borrower may default
- to compensate for the trouble involved in making the loan. Lending involves some administrative work on the part of the lender in terms of paperwork, recording of transactions, recovery costs and the like.
- and as payment for the use of money over the period of the loan.

Question 10

(c) What factors determine the level of interest rates in an economy? Illustrate your answer with diagrams.

MODEL ANSWER:

Theories of interest are usually divided into *classical* and *modern* theories.

According to *classical theory* the rate of interest is determined by the supply and demand for loanable funds. The rate of interest in equilibrium will be determined by the interaction of supply and demand for loanable funds. The *supply of* loanable funds comes from household and firms who have excess funds; that is funds that are not required for current expenditure. The *demand for* loanable funds arises because capital is productive – the productivity of capital will more than compensate the entrepreneur for the loss involved in paying interest. **Figure 5.8** illustrates the equilibrium situation.

Figure 5.8

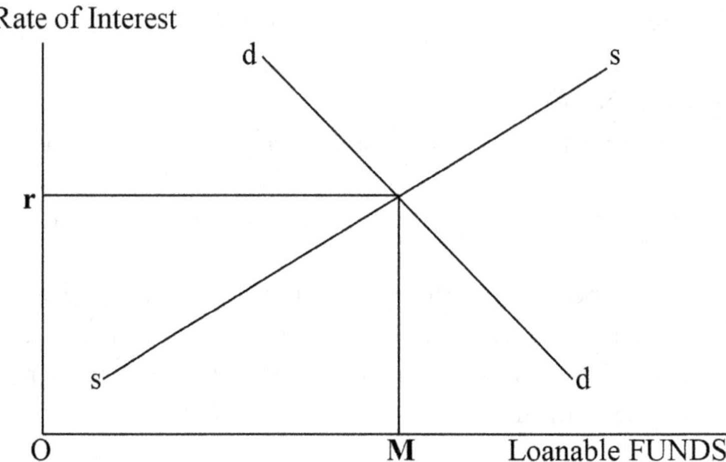

As an explanation of interest rate determination, classical theory suffers from a number of defects:

- it does not explain why government policy can influence interest rates as often happens in practice.

- under classical assumptions saving and investment would be fairly stable. Thus, the theory fails to explain short term variations in interest rates that are often observed in the real world.

- the theory assumes that all income that is saved is automatically lent out. However, apart from being reluctant to save, individuals may be reluctant to lend.

Modern theories of interest rate determination are based on the **liquidity preference** theory. Liquidity preferences refer to people's preferences for holding liquid assets as opposed to interest earning assets such as bonds. A change in liquidity preference or demand for money relative to bonds will cause the rate of interest to change. Thus, if it becomes less attractive to hold money, people will buy bonds and the rate of interest will fall. Conversely, if it becomes attractive to hold money, people will move out of bonds into cash and the rate of interest will rise. **Figure 5.9** shows the liquidity preference schedule (Ly). This shows the amount of money that the public wishes to hold according to the rate of interest being offered. It is assumed that the supply of money is under the control of the government. We now wish to examine the effect of a shift in the money supply by assuming that this increases from OM1 to OM2 in the diagram. From the diagram, we can see that this will result in a fall in the interest rate from r1 to r2. The same diagram can be used to show that a decrease in the money supply (say from OM2-OM1) will cause the rate of interest to rise.

Figure 5.9

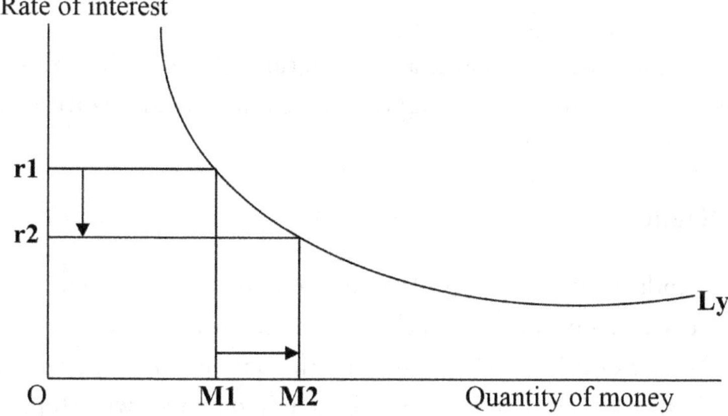

6 Public Finance, Money and Banking

Question 1

(a) *What are the main arguments for and against ownership and operation of an industry by the State as opposed to the private sector?*

MODEL ANSWER:

Arguments for state ownership and operation of industries are often made on economic and social grounds. The arguments in **favour** of state ownership are as follows:

Public Sector

* Some industries are not profitable from the point of view of the private sector but are nevertheless essential for national survival. In the absence of private sector funding, the only method of preserving such industries is for the state to take them into public ownership. This is over and above other public goods. [Public goods are those goods or services which cannot be produced by private firms because it is impossible to produce them just for only one person. These goods and services are consumed by everybody; in general they are produced by state enterprises].

* Certain industries are cheaper to operate as monopolies. Such industries are known as *natural monopolies.* These industries include those dealing with milk processing, water supplies, electricity, telephones and internet infrastructure. In such industries, competition between private enterprise firms would result in an unnecessary duplication of capital.

It is argued that state ownership of such industries prove beneficial by taking advantage of economies of scale and thus reducing operating costs. Where a natural monopoly exists, monopoly production will often be the cheapest form of operation.

* State ownership is often motivated by the desire to provide a universal service to all the citizens of the country. It enables the industry to make the service available at reasonable price even to remote communities where small scale operation can be extremely costly. Sometimes the service is supplied at a financial loss. This argument has been used in many countries to support the provision of postal, telephone, rail and electricity services to remote parts of the country.

* It is also argued that under state ownership workers will enjoy better working conditions. Because the state is the owner of the enterprise and not a private firm striving to maximize profits, workers' morale will be high and this will be reflected in increased output.

* Some industries provide a scarce public resource, which is limited in the range of its effectiveness or capacity, to the community. Where governments are directly involved as providers, it is argued that state ownership allows the resource to be rationed fairly. An example is radio and television broadcasting where, if private sector entry were not restricted, airwaves would be crowded and interference between individual broadcasters' transmissions would undermine the quality of the reception.

* A final argument is that certain industries (for example, those producing armaments, iron and steel, power, and so on) are essential to the nation's well-being. For this reason, they should be owned and operated by the state in the national interest, especially as regards the maintenance of a high level of employment, security and defense.

Question 1

(b) Present arguments against state ownership.

MODEL ANSWER:

Private Sector

The main arguments advanced **against** state ownership of an industry but those that favour the private sector are as follows:

* By restricting the operation of the free market mechanism, it leads to inefficiency. One source of inefficiency is the bureaucracy. Because state owned corporations tend to be very large, this complicates the task of management. The vast amounts of paperwork and the complex legal proceedings impede the corporation's ability to respond quickly to changing economic conditions. Under private enterprise, profits and competition acts as spur to efficiency.

* State ownership also leads to a reduction in consumer choice. If the consumer is dissatisfied with the commodity or service provided by the state owned enterprise there is no-one else to turn to. Under private enterprise this problem is not serious because there is usually a large number of competing enterprises.

* In some cases industries that are owned by the state such as the National Railways of Zimbabwe (NRZ) or Zambia Railways (ZR) have made substantial losses. These losses have to be paid for by the taxpayer even if they are the consequence of inefficient management. Zambia Airways (ZA) went bankrupt and folded because of excessive losses as a result of shoddy management.

* At one point many of Zambia's private companies and mining operations were nationalized. Those in mining were grouped under the umbrella of ZIMCO (such as ZCCM & RST) or INDECO if they were involved in industrial or manufacturing activities. This was the theme during the *one-party* (socialist oriented) regime. This picture changed as soon as multiparty politics was validated and

democracy emerged. Then, a more liberal economic system was ushered in which had a preference for private enterprise.

Question 2

(a) Define National Debt.

MODEL ANSWER:

The National Debt is defined as the cumulative total of outstanding government borrowing over the years. The state can borrow from both domestic and international markets.

Question 2

(b) What factors determine the level of interest rates in an economy? Illustrate your answer with diagrams.

MODEL ANSWER:

The answer to this question depends on the method used to finance the national debt. The government has essentially four main ways/methods of doing this:

- Through increasing taxation
- By borrowing from internal sources
- By borrowing from external sources
- By printing money.

The implications of each method of financing are discussed below.

* *Increasing taxation:* Households and firms are taxed. In this case the consumer's disposable income is reduced and thus his/her ability to purchase goods and services is diminished. The resources raised from

higher taxes are transferred to the government. For the nation as a whole, this method of financing involves no burden to the national economy. The citizens of the country suffer a fall in their disposable incomes but these resources are transferred to the government. The higher taxes may, however, discourage efforts by enterprises leading to a fall in output. If so, the debt could be said to constitute a burden to the economy.

* *Domestic borrowing:* In this case the people who lend money to the government suffer a reduction in consumption or production. Those who do not lend money to the government do not bear the current costs of increased government activity. However, unlike taxation, this method of financing the debt merely represents a transfer of resources from the private sector to the government and does not involve a burden for the nation as a whole. The only pain might be *crowding out*, if government borrows excessively.

* *Foreign borrowing:* If the debt is financed from foreign sources there is no need to reduce current consumption at home. However, eventually payment of interest and principal to those foreign lenders will give them a claim on the nation's resources. Note also that repayment of interest and principal may be transferred to future generations so it could be said that future generations bear the burden of the debt that was incurred by their ancestors. However, this is not strictly correct because future generations would enjoy the benefits generated by the project. Provided the money so borrowed was not embezzled, spent on consumption goods, or wasted on useless (so called white elephant) projects.

* *Printing money:* This method of financing will, in conditions of full employment, lead to inflation. Those on fixed incomes suffer a fall in real income but the government will obtain more resources for its own use. Thus, for the nation as a whole, this method of financing the debt does not impose a burden on the economy.

In conclusion, while the foregoing discussion would suggest that the national debt does not impose a burden on the national economy, it nevertheless needs to be emphasized that an increasing national debt involves higher interest payments and higher taxation levels. As already noted, high taxes may be a disincentive to effort and enterprise leading to a fall in output. Hence, restraint or some tax cuts are necessary to beef up the economy. Furthermore, as the size of the debt increases, so do the costs of servicing the debt. Zimbabwe and Zambia have over time gone through periods of HIPC (High Indebted Per Capita) distress.

Question 3

(a) Distinguish between ad valorem and specific taxes.

MODEL ANSWER:

Ad valorem taxes are those that are charged as a percentage of the value of the transaction. An 8% sales tax is an example of an *ad valorem* tax and means that 8% of the monetary value of anything sold or bought (and is subject to this tax) goes towards this tax. *Specific taxes* are those that are levied per unit or weight of the commodity, for example, $2 per kg of maize.

Question 3

(b) "Apart from raising revenue for the government, taxation serves a number of other economic and social functions." Discuss.

MODEL ANSWER:

Apart from raising revenue, taxation serves a number of other economic and social functions.

* It can be used to encourage the provision of goods and services that would not be easily or adequately catered for by private enterprise. Such goods are known as *public goods* and include defense, law and order, bridges and universal education. The government raises revenue from taxation and provides public goods on a collective basis.

* Taxation can also be varied to influence domestic economic variables such as consumption, investment and saving as part of overall macro-economic policy. It can be used to discourage the consumption of goods that can cause harm. For example, the government can discourage the excessive consumption of alcohol and cigarettes by imposing a heavy sales tax on these goods or, alternatively, it can encourage the consumption of baby food by placing a subsidy on all sales of baby food. If demand is elastic, more will be purchased after the imposition of the subsidy.

* The government can also use taxation to achieve greater equality of income and wealth. Levying more taxes on high income earners is in effect a form of distribution of income. This policy helps to reduce the gap between rich and poor people. When the tax system is progressive, as is the case in Zimbabwe and many African countries, the income differences remaining after increased taxation will be significantly less than those that existed before the imposition of the tax.

* Taxation can also be used to promote economic growth -- since an increase in taxation can be a disincentive to effort and enterprise thus reducing the levels of economic growth, the opposite effect will be achieved with a reduction in taxation.

If the government wants to increase economic incentives it can do so by reducing the levels of taxation. In order to create jobs, taxes paid by private enterprises, especially small and medium sized ones can be reduced to good effect on job creation. Other measures to promote economic growth include the taxation of distributed profits at a higher rate than retained profits. Companies can also be given generous investment allowances on say capital equipment that are financed out of taxation. The effect of both these measures would be to lower costs of production for firms and raise the level of investment in the economy.

* In regional policy, taxation can be used to influence the location of industry. Tax allowances or concessions can be given to firms to

encourage them to locate in areas suffering high levels of unemployment. For example, tax incentives are often used to encourage companies such as Banks to open branches in rural or remote places.

* Taxation can also be used for fiscal stabilization purposes. Taxes are a leakage from the circular flow of income. Thus, if the government wishes to reduce the level of economic activity, it can do so by increasing the level of taxes.

From this discussion, it can thus be seen that apart from raising revenue, *taxation* serves a large number of other economic and social functions. For example, Canada's equalization policy (a form of taxation), riches provinces – such as oil-rich Alberta, send money through Federal Government, to poorer ones like Quebec and Nova Scotia; so that Canadians get comparable level of public services regardless of where they live.

Question 4

(a) What are externalities?

MODEL ANSWER:

Broadly speaking, externalities are the incidental benefits or costs of an economic activity which affects persons whom the market does not compensate or charge for the cost or the benefit produced by the activity. That is, the cost or benefit does not fall on the persons directly involved in the activity. These externalities can be beneficial or harmful. The beautification of a site where a dam has been constructed is an example of a beneficial externality while the pollution of an area resulting from production activity in a factory is an example of a harmful externality. Toxic effluents discharged into a river providing drinking water is a dangerous or costly externality.

Question 4

(b) What are the consequences of externalities?

MODEL ANSWER:

The presence of an externality will cause the costs arising from a firm's activity to diverge from the social opportunity costs of the activity. In such situations, the free market mechanism will lead to a misallocation of resources.

This can be explained as follows. A private firm engaged in production will only take into account the marginal private costs (MPC) of production. However, for society as a whole, the relevant costs to consider are the marginal social costs of production (MSC). These costs are defined as:

MSC = MPC + the incidental costs (XC) that are borne by people other than those engaged in that particular activity.

Note that the incidental costs can be negative (harmful externality) or positive (beneficial externality).

In other words, what this definition says is that for the private profit-maximizing firm MPC = MB, where MPC is defined as before and (MB) is the marginal benefit of the activity of the firm. This means that when a *harmful externality* is present, MSC will be greater than MPC and smaller outputs than those currently being produced by the firm will be *socially optimal*. On the other hand, when the activity is *beneficial* to society we find that MB is greater than MSC. In this case, larger outputs than those currently being produced will be socially optimal. **Figure 6.1** illustrates the nature of the problem for a harmful externality. The firm's profit maximizing output is found where MPC=MR at 0Qm (point A). But with a harmful externality, the relevant marginal cost curve from society's point of view is the one labeled MSC. In this case, the firm should reduce output to the level shown by OQsoc (point

B) because the benefits of producing this output exceed the costs of producing these units.

Figure 6.1

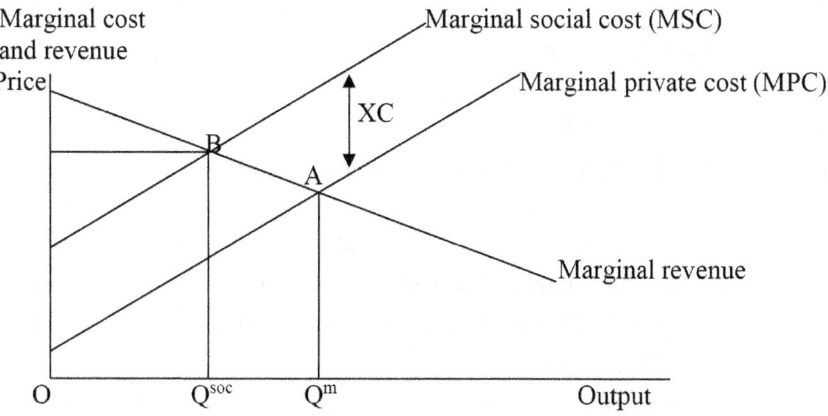

Explained another way, this implies that goods and services that come with ***negative externalities,*** which are costly to third parties, end up being overproduced. This is primarily because firms do not take into account these costs when they produce. As an example, since no individual person owns the river, a nearby plant can pollute the river at will, worrying only about its private costs of raw materials and other operational costs. Whereas, if someone owned the river, the firm would be charged for the harm caused by its effluents. Therefore, firms normally take a *free ride* socially because there is no mechanism in the free market system for taking these pollution costs into account.

Figure 6.1 also shows the consequences to society when firms *overproduce goods and services.* Assuming unchanged demand curves, as the producer shifts his supply curve, the exact amount of overproduction expected and how much harm is caused by each unit of overproduction can be determined. In **Figure 6.1,** the lower supply curve captures only the marginal private costs (MPC) of the firm. While the upper curve takes into account not only the firm's private costs but also the *incidental external pollution costs* (XC). Hence, the *marginal social costs* (MSC) curve captures all costs associated with producing the firm's goods and services.

Question 4

(c) *Describe some of the measures that the government can take to deal with the problem of externalities.*

MODEL ANSWER:

The problem of negative externalities can be tackled by:

- Imposing suitable taxes or subsidies. For example, if a firm's activities have harmful side effects, the government can impose a tax or pay the firm a subsidy equal to the difference between MSC and MPC. Imposing taxes (say, a charge or cost for each ton of pollution emitted) on firms generating negative externalities might discourage polluting behavior.

- Making use of direct regulation. This might entail passing laws, banning or restricting the method of production used, or adopting measures to influence the location of the polluting firm or outright prohibition.

- Passing laws which directly target the negative externality itself rather than the underlying activity – such as installation of smokestacks or filters in factories.

In practice, dealing with the problem of externalities is complicated. For example, it is always difficult to value social costs and benefits in money terms. However, such valuations would be required to estimate the amount of tax or subsidy to be imposed.

Question 5

(a) Using an example, discuss the consequences of positive externalities.

MODEL ANSWER:

Positive externalities (benefits) occur when goods and services provide positive externalities to third parties. The output of these tends to be under produced. A good example is a ***Bee Keeper*** who produces honey for the market. But the same bees he relies on to produce honey end up pollinating the flowers of local farmers who consume honey from the beekeeper as well.

Because local farmers do not pay the beekeeper for his bees pollinating their fields, the beekeeper has no incentive to produce extra units of honey. Therefore, he contents himself with the use of fewer beehives (low output). **Figure 6.2** illustrates this situation.

Figure 6.2

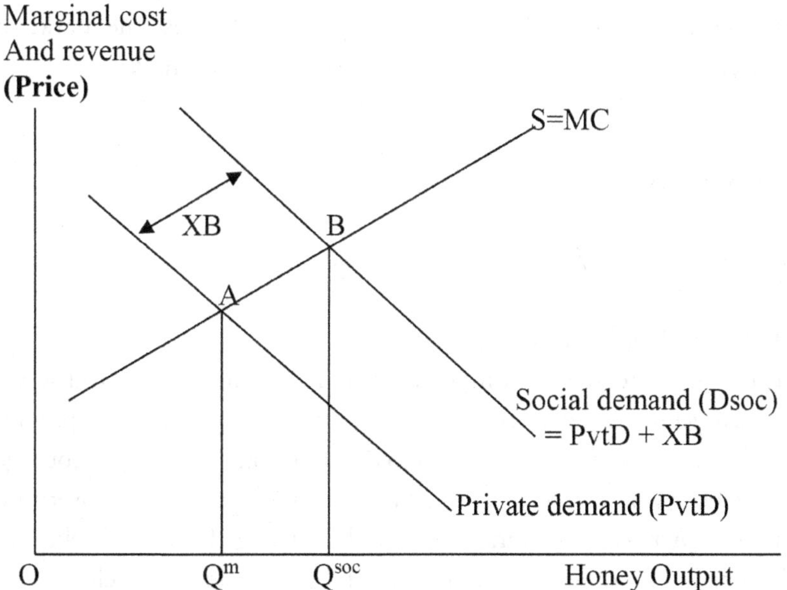

Where: XB = external benefits;
Dsoc = new social demand;
PvtD = private demand;

In **Figure 6.2**, the beekeeper's supply curve is the marginal cost curve (MC) labeled S = MC. The demand for honey paid for by customers is the private demand curve (PvtD). Where the supply curve (MC) intersects private demand (PvtD) [point A] the *market equilibrium quantity* of honey (OQ^m) is attained.

But this output does not take into account the *benefits of bees* pollinating the farmers' fields. When you shift the private demand curve (PvtD) to include also *external benefits* (XB), the new social demand curve (Dsoc) intersects supply curve at a higher social quantity (OQ^{soc}). These benefits are defined as: Dsoc = PvtD + XB or social demand is equal to private demand ***plus*** the incidental extra benefits (XB) that accrue to farmers other than the utility they obtain from consuming honey.

That way, honey production benefits **both** the beekeeper and the local farmers at the *socially optimal output level* of OQ^{soc}. At this level each unit of output, the *total social benefit* is at least as great as the beekeeper's *cost of production*. At OQ^m (point A) the market equilibrium output is smaller than the socially optimal output OQ^{soc} (point B), because the market has no mechanism to take into account these positive externalities.

Question 5

(b) Explain a way of dealing with positive externality.

MODEL ANSWER:

Because of the tendency of markets to under-produce goods and services that have *positive externalities,* one method to increase these is to provide a *subsidy* (i.e. a payment) to producers so that more output can be encouraged. A beekeeper would receive a monetary incentive /grant from government so that he increases the number of hives he is using. That is, a beekeeper is subsidized to produce more honey, which by extension also helps farmers. To raise or recoup some of this subsidy money – government may decide to levy or tax the local farmers.

Another example of a positive externality can arise when a municipal government plants lots of trees in a city. The improvement of air quality resulting from these trees, apart from them enhancing the beauty of the landscape, is a positive externality.

Question 6

(a) Discuss cost and Benefit Analysis.

MODEL ANSWER:

Cost Benefit Analysis

Cost Benefit Analysis (or CBA for short) describes a method of assessing the relative merits of a large scale investment projects. It examines the worth of projects from a societal point of view. That is, it attempts to enumerate all the relevant costs and benefits from the point of view of society as a whole. In this respect, the approach that takes CBA considerations into account differs from that of a private firm which would take into account only the private costs and benefits of the project. Hence, the CBA approach is much broader and involves a consideration of economic, political as well as social factors.

Question 6

(b) What are the main principles of CBA?

MODEL ANSWER:

General Principles of CBA

As already noted, CBA is used to make decisions on whether a particular project is *socially worthwhile* or not. This assists the decision maker in choosing from a number of alternative projects. This approach differs from that of a private firm in a number of ways. *First,* when a private firm assesses the relative worth of alternative projects, it typically begins by examining the technical feasibility of the projects. The *second stage* is to compare the estimated stream of revenues with costs over the estimated life of the project. The *final stage* is to estimate how much of each alternative will contribute to the profits of the firm by subtracting total costs from total benefits. CBA is designed to deal with much of the same problem but the analysis differs in the following aspects:

- Private sectors decisions are made to enhance the interests of shareholders but the CBA approach takes a much broader view by taking into account the interests of society as a whole.

- The valuation of costs and benefits using a CBA yardstick is much more difficult because some of these elements are intangible and certain outputs of public investment projects are provided free to the public and hence are not given any market values.

- Market prices often do not reflect the true social costs and benefits of inputs and outputs; hence, under CBA, there is the need to make adjustments to take account of the market situation.

Given these considerations, the general principles of CBA must involve the following:

- How should these costs and benefits be valued?

- What constraints need to be considered?

In the following sections, we try to clarify some of these valuation issues.

Question 6

(c) What are some of the valuation concerns related to CBA?

MODEL ANSWER:
The Main Issues related to Valuation

- *Enumeration of costs and benefits*: To begin with, the scope and nature of the project being analyzed must be defined (for example, new school or dam) to understand its relationship with existing projects.

- *Externalities:* The wider social costs and benefits of the projects should be considered in any CBA study and attempts should be made to quantify them. Externalities are defined as the benefits received or costs borne by those not associated with the activities. Examples of harmful externalities are noise and air pollution resulting from production activity in a factory. In the private sector, firms aim to maximize private profits, therefore such costs are generally ignored. In CBA, all externalities (positive or negative) should be taken into account.

- *Project life*: the life of the project should be estimated based on an assessment of the physical length of life of the project and technological changes it will engender and so on.

- *Valuation of Social Costs and Benefits*: Where costs and prices can be expressed in money terms adjustments need to be made in respect of anticipated price changes of future inputs and expected changes in interest rates over time. Normally, market prices are used to value social costs and benefits. However, when monopolistic elements exist in the market for goods and factors of production, market prices will be distorted. Similarly, the wages of workers may contain a rent element in excess of marginal product of the workers. When distortions in the market prices are present, adjustments need to be made to make prices reflect the true cost of the product or factors of production. Such adjusted prices are known as *shadow prices*. In addition, most economists prefer to measure input prices at factor costs, that is, taxes are deducted and subsidies are added.

- *Collective goods*: Market prices cannot be used to value the costs and benefits of goods that are not sold on the market. A good example is a public good like a bridge. The quantity of public goods that are available is usually a byproduct of the political process. One possible solution to this problem is to estimate the full cost of providing these goods and then decide whether this cost is justified in the light of the benefits expected from the project.

Another approach would be to use the prices of comparable goods and services in the private sector as an estimate of the true cost of providing these goods and services.

- *Intangible items:* These pose problems which are similar to collective goods in that they cannot be quantified. An example would be the valuation of lives lost during the construction of a dam site. In CBA, every attempt should be made to include intangible items in the valuation of costs and benefits. An estimate of the costs to be used could be based on questionnaires to consumers to determine how much they would be prepared to pay for the item in question.

- *Choice of discount rate*: In this case, a decision has to be made as to which discount rate should be used when discounting the costs and benefits. There are *two main rates* to choose from:

    * The social discount rate – which is the government borrowing rate.

    * The social opportunity cost rate – which is based on the opportunity cost of the resources invested in the project from the point of view of society as a whole.

Whichever rate is finally chosen will have repercussions on the project chosen and the choice of techniques, that is, whether to use capital intensive or labour intensive techniques of production. The larger the discount rate, the smaller the present value of future costs and benefits.

Question 6

(d) What are some of the limitations related to CBA?

MODEL ANSWER:

The Constraints related to CBA

There are five main constraints to consider as follows:

- *Physical*: For example, is there sufficient land available for the project? Can the equipment chosen do the job within the time required?

- *Legal:* Needless to say, the project being considered and the ways of bringing it to fruition should be within the framework of the law.

- *Administrative constraints:* There may be limits as to how much work can be handled administratively.

- *Budgeting:* How much capital/funding is available for the project and whether it is sufficient to cover the cost of the planned project.

- *Distributional:* The distributional effects of the project should also be considered. As a result of undertaking the project there may well be beneficiaries and losers. For example, property values may go down following the construction of a hydro-electric plant in a particular area or land may be expropriated in order to make room for the highway project being considered.

- *Uncertainty:* It is also necessary to take into account risks and uncertainty when making the choice of project. The methods used to assess risk and uncertainty, however, lie beyond the scope of this book.

Summary of CBA approach

CBA is a method of assessing the social worth of a project for society as a whole. It is based on comparative analyses of the social costs and benefits of a public investment project. To conduct a CBA study, the analyst should proceed as follows:

- Identify the problem, clarify the issues and then set out the terms and reference.
- Clearly define and set out the objectives of the proposed project.
- Outline all the alternatives that would achieve desired objectives.
- Identify the constraints that affect alternatives.

For each of the alternatives identified, proceed as follows:

- Make a list of the costs and benefits and then state the underlying assumptions.
- Quantify the costs and benefits.
- Compare the costs and benefits and then rank the projects according to their benefit/cost ratio (i.e., relating benefits to costs).
- Finally, the project with the highest benefit/cost ratio is selected. This procedure is illustrated in **Table 6.1** for a project with 3 alternatives A, B and C.

Table 6.1

Project	Benefits	Costs	B-C	B/C ratio	Rank
A	**600**	**500**	**100**	**1.2**	**2**
B	**700**	**600**	**100**	**1.16**	**3**
C	**950**	**750**	**250**	***1.26***	1

From Table 6.1 project C would be selected because it has the highest B/C ratio.

Question 7

(a) What are the main components of money supply in a country like Zimbabwe or Zambia?

MODEL ANSWER:

The total money supply in Zimbabwe or Zambia consists of the following components.

- *M1:* the narrow definition of money. This consists of notes and coins in circulation and the demand for notes and coins in circulation and the demand deposits held with the monetary banking sector.

- *M2:* the broad definition. This compromises M1 + short dated savings and fixed deposits with the commercial banks.

Question 7

(b) Explain how the Reserve Bank of Zimbabwe or Bank of Zambia controls the money supply.

MODEL ANSWER:

The Central or Reserve Bank in a country can use the following methods to control the money supply.

- *Changing the Central Bank Discount Rate:* This is the interest rate at which the Reserve Bank/Central Bank lends money to commercial banks. Increases in *this rate* discourages such borrowing and forces commercial banks needing extra cash to obtain this cash by selling securities or liquidating loans. Decreases in this rate make borrowing by commercial banks cheaper and therefore encourages credit expansion.

Changes in the Central or Reserve Bank discount rate signal the general trend in interest rates and the fluidity or tightness of credit conditions. When this rate changes, so do the rates charged by commercial banks to customers. Thus, increases in this rate will cause banks lending to the private sector to contract. Conversely, the higher cost of funds makes it less attractive to borrow from the private sector. From the private sector's point of view, *higher interest rates* make it more attractive for them to lend to other private sector entities rather than investing the money themselves. Both of these trends tend to reduce the money supply.

- *Statutory Reserves and Liquidity Requirements*: To ensure the stability of the country's banking and financial system the Central or Reserve Bank insists that the monetary banking system hold a certain proportion of their assets in liquid form. By law, the liquid assets held by Banks must not fall below a certain level which is given as the *liquid asset ratio.* If the Reserve Bank/Central Bank increases the liquid asset ratio this increases the commercial banks' ability to lend. Conversely, if this ratio is reduced this decreases the commercial banks' ability to lend (and hence will cause a reduction in the money supply).

The commercial banks are also required to hold certain statutory reserves in the form of **deposits** with the Reserve or Central Banks. An increase in the statutory reserve ratio reduces the banks' ability to lend, a decrease increases it.

- *Open market operations:* If the Central or Reserve Bank wishes to increase the cash reserves of the commercial banks it can do so by purchasing securities on the open market. The procedure works as follows:

If the Central or Reserve Bank buys securities from the public, it pays for them by a cheque drawn on itself. The seller deposits the cheque in his bank account. The commercial bank will present this cheque to the Reserve/Central Bank for payment and its deposits at the Reserve/Central Bank will increase, thus permitting it to expand credit. Conversely, if the Reserve/Central Bank wishes to reduce the cash reserves of the commercial banks it sells securities on the open market. The Reserve/Central Bank receives a cheque from the purchaser and presents it to his bank for payment. When the cheque is cashed, the commercial bank's reserves at the Reserve/Central Bank will be reduced as will its ability to expand credit.

- *Moral suasion:* The Central or Reserve Bank can issue a direct request to the banking sector to reduce their lending. While commercial banks are allowed some degree of discretion in conforming to these requirements, the Reserve/Central Bank's request is usually taken seriously. This method has proved effective in controlling the money supply in the country.

Question 8

(a) What are the functions of money?

MODEL ANSWER:

Money is any generally acceptable medium of exchange. Money performs several functions in an economic system.

- *As Medium of Exchange:* Because money is generally acceptable it allows people to purchase goods and services. Specialization and division of labour only become possible in a money economy. Money makes it possible to run a modern system of exchange. It provides a basis for keeping accounts, calculating profit and loss and so on. Without money, people would have to exchange goods for goods – i.e. make use of a barter system.

- *As Store of Value:* Money is a useful way of storing purchasing power. A person can sell goods and keep the money until he needs it. To perform this function satisfactorily, it is essential that money has a stable value. Thus during rapid inflation the usefulness of money as a store of value diminishes because inflation reduces the purchasing power of money.

- *As Unit of Account and Standard of Deferred Payment*:

Society uses money as a yardstick for measuring the relative value of goods. It is also used as a standard of deferred payments. Loans are made and future contracts are fixed in terms of a monetary unit.

Question 8

(b) Discuss the problems of barter.

MODEL ANSWER:

Barter is the exchange of goods for goods. The problems of using barter system are as follows:

- *It necessitates a double coincidence of wants.* For example, if I want a car and I have 100 bags of maize, this means that I have to find someone who wants or needs bags of maize and has a car to exchange for the maize.

- *Barter is inefficient.* Time is wasted in looking for someone with suitable goods for exchange.

- When the goods involved are bulky *the system of barter is extremely cumbersome* especially when they have to be carried over a long distance.

- Under a *system of barter people are forced to be self-sufficient.* This reduces incentives to specialize.

7 Inflation, Investment and International Trade

Question 1

(a) Briefly describe inflation in economic terms.

MODEL ANSWER:

Simply put, the *inflation rate* is the measure of how the overall level of prices in the economy changes over time. Prices are rising if it is positive, and falling if the rate is negative. Thus, economists describe inflation as a situation where the general level of prices in the economy as a whole is rising. Although prices on few goods and services may fall, the large majority of prices rise. In general, price increases are associated with a growing, viable economy.

But when these price increases are larger than increases in productivity or real output, this causes an inflationary spiral which, if it persists, becomes a trend. Inflation can be classified by the factors causing it such as – demand-pull, cost-pull, or expectations-generated inflation. People dislike inflation because it reduces the purchasing power of money and nobody wants to pay higher prices. Also, with inflation, it becomes to predict how much money one needs to have or save for the future.

Question 2

(a) What are the different types of inflation and the consequences of each case?

MODEL ANSWER:

As stated above, inflation can be defined as a general or sustained increase in the price level. In an open economy, the following factors may give rise to inflation.

- *Excess demand in the home economy (demand-pull inflation):* If at the full employment level of output aggregate demand exceeds the capacity of the economy to produce goods and services this will exert upward pressure on the level of prices.

With *demand-pull inflation* - excessive aggregate demand may increase due to an increase in investment, government spending, autonomous consumption, and money supply; or decreases in taxes or saving. This is illustrated in **Figure** 7.1 where: **AD** = aggregate demand, **AS** = aggregate supply, **P** = general price level, and **GDP** = real output (gross domestic product).

Figure 7.1

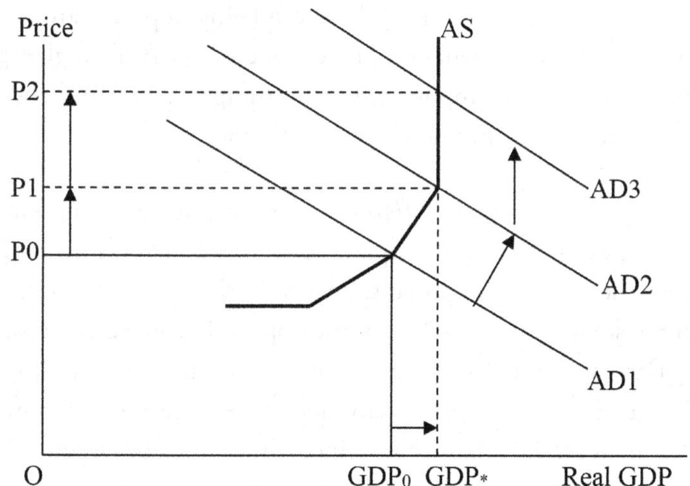

Demand-pull Inflation

Where: AS = aggregate supply; AD = aggregate demand; GDP = real output; P = general price level.

As illustrated in the diagram **Figure 7.1**, a right-hand shift in the aggregate demand curve (AD), from AD1 to AD2, increases both prices (P) and real output (GDP) in the short term. Thus, prices rise from P0 to P1 and GDP moves from GDP0 to GDP*. But as income levels increase, the *demand* for goods and services will also naturally rise. Initially, when demand increases, prices are bid up, which leads to output increase and the need for more workers to produce more products and services. But as resources are fully employed and aggregate demand (AD) continues to rise from AD2 to AD3, there is no more increase in GDP. Then prices rise from P1 to P2. This is what is known as *demand-pull inflation*, unanswered demand for goods and services expressing itself as shortages.

The remedy for this type of inflation or the expected response calls for a meaningful reduction in government spending and the money supply.

- *Imported inflation:* This refers to inflation that originates from other countries. For instance, suppose that country A is experiencing a demand pull inflation and country B is a major importer of goods from country A, then some of country A's inflation may be imported into country B. If the goods being imported are essential inputs into the production process of country B the higher prices being paid for the inputs will feed through to its firms' costs and prices thus worsening the initial inflation.

- *Cost push (or supply) inflation:* These results from autonomous increases in the costs of inputs, such as labour and raw materials, into the production process. The cost of borrowing, reflected by interest rates, may also have some impact. In some cases, cost push inflation may have its origins in demand-pull inflation, that is, input prices may rise initially due to demand pull pressures but the increase in prices is sustained through trade union pressure for higher wages to compensate for the initial rise in the cost of living. If these wage demands are granted, this will force producers to increase prices to compensate for the higher wage costs which will lead to union demands for even higher wages. In this way, the inflationary spiral will be kept in motion.

Cost-push inflation is illustrated in **Figure 7.2** below.

Figure 7.2

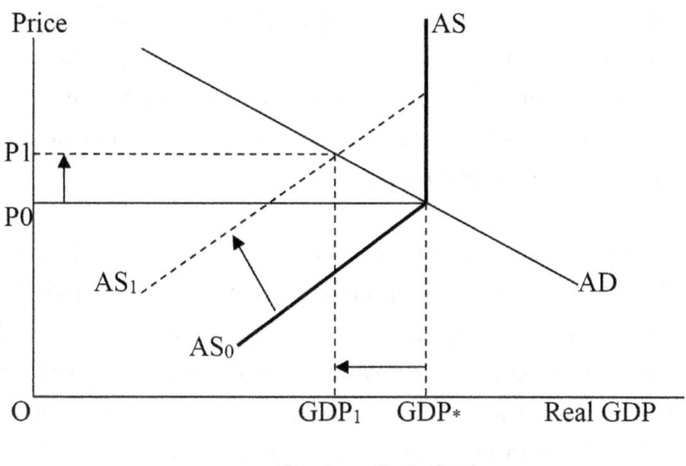

Cost-push Inflation

Higher costs of supply bring about an increase in the price (P) from P0 to P1 and a reduction in real output (GDP) from GDP* to GDP_1. In the long-run however, firms will be able to reduce wages because of higher levels of unemployment in the economy. This causes output to eventually return to its original (full employment) level at GDP*.

Unlike demand-pull inflation, cost-push inflation has no simple remedy.

- *Expectational inflation:* This arises due to trade union expectations of future inflation rates. Let us say that a trade union expects an inflation rate of 10% per annum during the following year. If so, they will use this figure as a base for their negotiations, in an effort to try and preserve the purchasing power of their wages. If the increase is granted on a country wide basis then the expectations of inflation will tend to be self-fulfilling. Namely, as wages increase because workers expect inflation, costs to firms increase. But in turn, these costs are passed on to consumers in form of higher prices.

- *Monetary causes:* According to Monetarists, inflation is "always and everywhere a monetary phenomenon." By this they mean that every inflation has as its root cause excessive monetary expansion. Monetarists disagree that wage push can be an independent cause of inflation. Their analysis of the causes of inflation is based on the Quantity Theory of Money and statistical studies which show a correlation between changes in the money supply and changes in the rate of inflation. (Quantity Theory) of Money states that the overall level of prices in the economy is proportional to the quantity of money circulating.

- *Structural rigidity inflation:* This theory assumes that resources do not move quickly enough from one use to another. Given these conditions, when patterns of demand and costs change, firms in expanding industries may experience shortages while those in contracting sectors will not be utilizing their capacity fully. Prices in expanding sectors will therefore rise while prices in contracting sectors will remain constant. This means that, on average, inflation will rise.

Question 2

(b) In a summary form what are the consequences of inflation?

MODEL ANSWER:

Consequences of inflation: These can be summarized as follows:

* During periods of inflation the attractiveness of money as a store of value diminishes. As a result, individuals may store increasing amounts of their wealth in the form of goods, such as precious stones, real estate, and jewelry. The quality of capital, in the form of physical goods, may deteriorate because those resources which are diverted from socially productive purposes lie idle.

* Changes in inflation impose costs on firms due to the need to revise prices every time there is a change in the inflation rate. Time may be wasted in negotiations with unions for higher wages to compensate workers for price changes.

* Inflation redistributes income from lenders to borrowers. The real value of borrowed money diminishes with every increase in the inflation rate. Thus part of the reason why banks charge interest rates on borrowed money is to compensate for a possible reduction in the real value of money due to inflation.

* Those on fixed incomes such as pensioners and owners of government bonds suffer because the real value of these securities falls as the rate of inflation increases. The poor groups in society seem to be hurt less by inflation than the rich ones who lose value on their assets as inflation sours the money market.

* With rising inflation, interest rates are likely to increase because lenders increase the rate of interest to compensate for the fall in the real value of their money. Note that rising interest rates will increase the cost of borrowing, deter investment and economic growth.

* If prices are rising this makes a country's exports uncompetitive, relative to those of other countries, causing deterioration in the country's terms of trade.

Question 3

(a) A special case of inflation is: Hyperinflation.
(i) can you briefly define it?
(ii) what are its consequences?

MODEL ANSWER:

(i) Hyperinflation: refers to inflation which is out of control because it is too high. In many developed Western economies, inflation in the range of 20 – 35% is considered hyperinflation. However many African countries

have experienced excessively high inflations. In recent times Zimbabwe has been a worst case scenario of hyperinflation, with the problem hitting hundreds and thousands of percentage.

In general, it is believed that a major causer for inflation is a money supply that grows too quickly. This implies that a remedy to inflation (slowing or stopping it) would be halting the growth of the money supply. Government printing a lot of money to pay for, say, budget deficits exacerbates inflation, causing prices to go up. On the other hand, printing too little money could also cause deflation which results in prices going down.

MODEL ANSWER:

(ii) Some *impacts/consequences* of hyperinflation:

* Hyperinflation causes major economic collapse resulting in high unemployment levels and a drastic decrease in the production of goods and services. Zimbabwe is a classical case many economists cite for hyperinflation. In 2008, the real GDP growth was a negative sixteen (-16.6%) percent.

* It destroys the incentive to save because everyone wants to spend his/her money as quickly as possible, fearing that it will continue losing value. Money is worth less every passing minute.

* It ruins the investment climate. That is, investment in business operations is discouraged. Foreign Direct Investments (FDI) dries up. When people do not save, there is no pool of money which can be used or borrowed for new investments. Economy slows down or stops growing, if there are no new investments or purchase of capital.

* In a hyperinflationary situation, people tend to be distracted because they are financially insecure and are doing their best to fashion strategies to shield themselves from the highly negative impact of a currency that is rapidly losing purchasing power.

Question 4

(a) What is the distinction between Phillips Curve and stagflation?

MODEL ANSWER:

(i) Phillips Curve is the inverse relationship between inflation and unemployment. Using empirical and other historical data, some economists, notably A.W. Phillips, Paul Samuelson and Robert Solow, have convincingly demonstrated that there is an inverse relationship between inflation and unemployment. That is, it has been shown that high inflation is generally associated with low unemployment rates and vice versa. This downward-sloping relationship between the *inflation rate* and the *unemployment rate* is commonly known as **Phillips Curve**. This is illustrated in **Figure 7.3** where: PC is the level of prices.

Figure 7.3

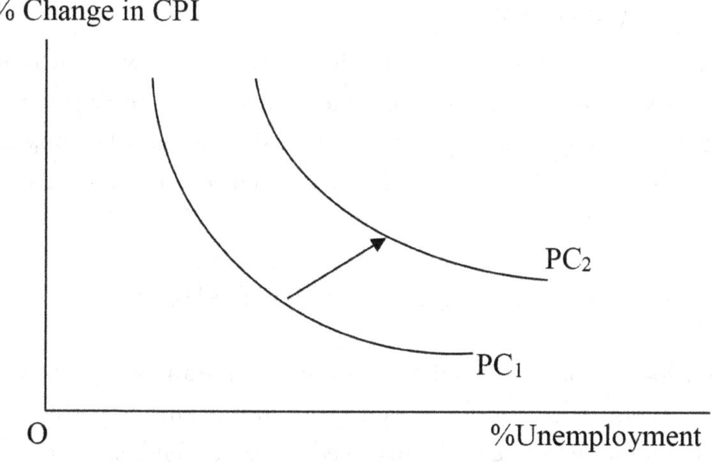

(ii) Stagflation becomes evident when inflation and unemployment occur *at the same time*. This complicates the job of policy makers who have to weigh the goals between price stability (keeping inflation in check), full employment (using all employable labour), and growth (economic expansion). In this situation, policy makers must therefore consider trade-offs, especially between unemployment and inflation. For example, a

policy leaning towards the Keynesian model would seek to attain full employment through increased spending while, if need be, simultaneously using more of the money supply. But there must be awareness that this policy may in turn spark price increases (inflation).

But since in real economies the trade-offs between the unemployment rate and price pressures change over time, this causes shifts in the *Phillips Curve* either upward or downward. An upward shift (from PC1 to PC2 in **Figure 7.3** for example), may be caused by supply shocks. Therefore, unless the policy maker is fully alert to all possible dangers, the policy used may yield unintended results.

Question 5

(a) *What is indexation? Assess the case for and against the indexation of financial contracts such as wages, pensions, taxes and social security payments.*

MODEL ANSWER:

Indexation refers to a provision either in law or contract whereby monetary payments such as wages, pensions, taxes and social security payments are adjusted whenever there is a change in the inflation rate. The objective on indexation is to insulate the economy from some of the undesirable effects of inflation.

Several advantages are claimed for a system of indexing:

* It helps to avoid the maldistribution of income and wealth that usually accompanies inflation. For example, full indexing of pensions would alleviate some of the problems faced by older members of society who draw on pensions.

* It alleviates the misallocation of resources that results from inflation such as the gains that accrue to borrowers at the expense of lenders.

* It reduces some of the gains that accrue to the government as a result of inflation (inflation results in a reduction in the real value

of government debt). Because of this, the government has a greater incentive to fight inflation.

* Indexation eases wage-push pressures. This reduces trade union incentives to fight inflation thereby helping to improve the industrial relations climate.

Opponents of indexation point out that:

* It speeds up the response to inflationary disturbances. For example, following the response to inflationary shock such as an increase in the price of oil (which would be a once-and-for-all increase), this would feed through to the consumer price index which would, in turn, result in a sequence of upward movements in wages and prices. Thus, indexation has the effect of reinforcing the inherent downward flexibility of wages and prices in the economy.

* If indexation is practiced on an extensive scale, this will enable economic agents to adapt more quickly and easily to inflationary pressures. While this is sometimes regarded as an advantage, it does however reduce the incentive to tackle the root cause of inflation.

* In the case of wages, if the initial distribution of income between capital and labour is unfair, indexation does nothing to solve this basic problem.

Question 6

(a) Distinguish between an inflationary gap and a deflationary gap.

MODEL ANSWER:

An inflationary gap is defined as the extent to which the desired level of *aggregate demand* exceeds the *full employment level* of income (where aggregate demand is the total demand for goods and services in an economy and full employment amounts to a situation in which every worker who needs a job can get one). In the presence of an inflationary gap, aggregate demand should be reduced by the amount of the inflationary gap to bring down the rate of inflation.

A deflation gap is the amount by which aggregate demand must be reduced in order to achieve the *full employment level* of output. To increase the level of output, on the other hand, aggregate demand should be increased by the amount of the inflationary gap. The two concepts are illustrated in **Figure 7.4** and **Figure 7.5** respectively.

Figure 7.4

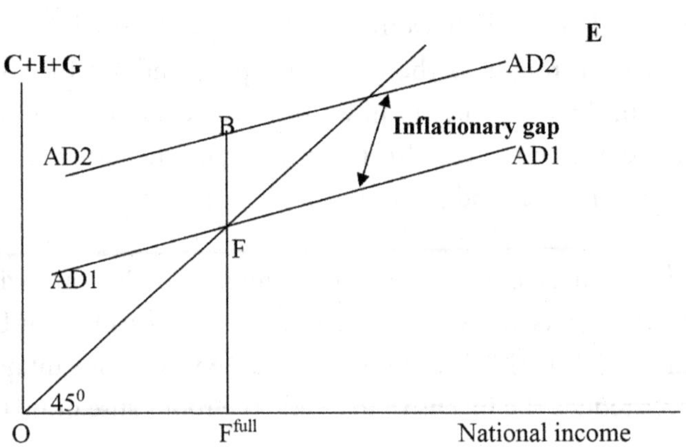

Figure 7.5

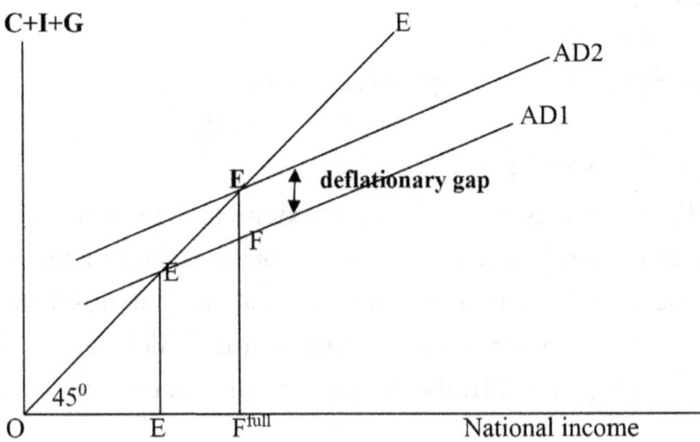

In **Figure 7.4**, AD1 and AD2 represent two different levels of aggregate demand. The full employment level of output is given by the intersection of the 45° line and the aggregate demand curve AD1 at F. The *inflationary gap* is given by the distance BF.

In **Figure 7.5**, the equilibrium level of income E is given by the intersection of the 45° line and the aggregate demand curve AD1. And the full employment level of national income is given by the intersection of the aggregate demand curve AD2 and the 45° degree line at F. The *deflationary gap* is given by the distance EF.

Question 7

(a) What are the economic arguments for and against income policies?

MODEL ANSWER:

Incomes policy aims to control the level of **wages** so as to preserve **price stability**. Although in theory incomes policies should apply to all incomes, encompassing wages, interest, rent and profit, in practice the policy is usually restricted to wages and salaries only as these account for a large proportion of people's incomes in most economies.

One major argument put forward in *favour* of an incomes policy is that it can have a major impact on inflationary expectations. This policy gives an indication of the government's determination to keep the rate of inflation under control. Expectations about inflation tend to be self-fulfilling and incomes policies help to keep these expectations under control.

The main arguments *against* incomes policies are as follows:

i) When they are voluntary, they may be largely ineffective because they ask workers and entrepreneurs to forgo one of their main objectives, namely the maximization of their incomes. Thus little co-operation can be expected from unions and businessmen when a voluntary incomes policy is in operation.

ii) Where incomes policies have the force of law they may be more effective. However, with the passage of time trade unions and employers may find ways of evading these regulatory controls.

iii) Economists who favour the operation of free market forces argue that incomes policies interfere with the allocation function of the price mechanism. An efficient allocation of resources requires that production and factor prices fluctuate freely in response to free market forces.

iv) Incomes policies prevent the economy from making such adjustments and distort production and distribution structures. Those who favour incomes policies, however, argue that it is possible to design an incomes policy that has sufficient flexibility to allow the price mechanism to operate efficiently.

v) Evidence from several countries indicates that where incomes policies have been implemented their effect on the rate of inflation has been only temporary. After the controls are abandoned, economic agents may expect the inflation rate to increase again. If so, incomes policies only serve to postpone the initial inflation.

vi) There is a danger that an incomes policy may operate in a discriminatory fashion. Some sectors of the economy may be easier to control than others and these sectors would bear the brunt of any incomes policy.

As far as Zimbabwe and Zambia are concerned -- the main thrust of policy positions as regards wages has been to raise the minimum level of incomes. For reasons associated with these countries' colonial history, wages for Africans were kept very low until they became independent in 1980 and 1964 respectively. Salaries at the top range of the executive scale are also controlled. However, these governments have not instituted any formal incomes policies as such.

Question 8

(a) Explain fully what you understand by the accelerator theory of investment.

MODEL ANSWER:
The *accelerator theory of investment* says that investment depends on the rate of change of national income rather than on its absolute change.

The theory can be explained as follows. Business investment consists of two elements. The first element is *replacement investment (*that is, depreciation). The second element is *net investment* (that is, additions to capital stock).

If entrepreneurs expect the demand for their goods and services to remain constant they need not add to their capital stock. If so, investment will be limited to replacing plant and equipment that has depreciated.

However, if entrepreneurs expect the level of demand for their products to increase, they will add to their capital stock of investment. We refer to this kind of investment as being induced. The significance of the induced nature of business investment is that when national income is rising (when sales are increasing) it is necessary to invest in more plant capacity. In addition, expectations based on the falling level of sales will be unfavorable.

The *accelerator theory* is shown in **Table 7.1** where we assume a *constant capital output ratio* of 1:2. For example, for year 1 the capital output ratio is 90/180=1.2. In year 2 sales increase to \$200m therefore the new level of required capital stock with an assumed capital output ratio of 1:2 is \$100m yielding the required additional investment of \$10m. In year 3, annual sales increase to \$240m and the additional investment required is \$20m. Between years 6 and 7 there is no change in sales so no additional investment is required. Note that in years 8-10 sales declines, therefore the required change in investment, is *negative.*

Table 7.1

Year	Annual Sales $M	Change in Sales	Required Capital Stock	Required Change in Investment
1	180	0	90	
2	200	20	100	+10
3	240	40	120	+20
4	300	60	150	+30
5	400	100	200	+50
6	420	20	210	+10
7	420	0	210	-
8	400	-20	200	-10
9	360	-40	180	-20
10	300	-60	150	-30

Where: capital output ratio = 1:2

Question 8

(b) Discuss the weaknesses of this theory as an explanation of investment behavior.

MODEL ANSWER:

As an explanation of investment behavior the *accelerator theory* suffers from a number of defects.

- It does not apply to investment to replace worn out equipment or to invest in new technology. It only applies to that part of total investment that increases the firm's capacity to produce goods and services. Thus, it does not apply to changes that are thought to be temporary.

- It does not apply when there is excess capacity in the industry. In such circumstances, firms will respond to an increase in demand by utilizing the excess capacity rather than adding to their capital stock.

- And, it ignores the fact that it takes time to increase capacity following a change in demand. The response of investment to a demand change may be spread over a long period of time. These lags imply that the rigid accelerator type relationship may not hold.

Question 9

(a) Define investment.

MODEL ANSWER:

Investment refers to the act of purchasing goods and services that are to be used for further production. In other words, firms need to spend to increase the economy's stock of capital as well as the value of their inventories. Investment is essential because firms need the capacity, in terms of stock, to be able to produce goods and services. Capital stock increases when firms spend on additions to plants, new equipment, machinery, computers, raw material inputs (or inventories) and other tools for producing goods and services.

As this capital stock wears out or becomes obsolete, or decreases in its value commonly referred to as depreciation, firms must make new investments in order to replace what is worn out or discarded.

Economists distinguish between several different types of investment as follows:

- *Fixed investment*: This refers to investment in fixed capital equipment. Demand for capital goods is derived demand in the sense that it arises from the increased demand for the firm's output.

Capital goods are not demanded for their own sake but for what they can produce.

- *Inventories:* These represent the purchase of finished products and raw materials which the firm keeps on hand to avoid the inconveniences of future shortages or to protect the firm from possible disruptions in supply.

- *Housing investment:* This represents investment in residential construction.

Question 9

(b) What are the main determinants of investment?

MODEL ANSWER:

Different types of investment are subject to different influences as the following examples illustrate.

- *Fixed investment:* As already noted, fixed investment is derived from the demand for the firm's output. This in turn depends on the adequacy of existing equipment -- its size and age. In this connection we distinguish between replacement investment and net investment. Replacement investment refers to investment to replace worn out equipment. Net investment refers to additions to the total capital stock.

- *Inventories:* The level of a firm's inventory is influenced among other things by the total level of its production. If production is increasing we expect firms to increase their stock of inventories and vice versa if production is falling.

- *Housing investment:* Investment in housing is influenced by various factors such as changes in population, the level of interest rates and National Income.

At a general level, the following factors are considered to be important determinants of investment. A firm will invest if its potential profits versus its costs, measured in terms of interest rates or the cost of borrowing money, is likely to yield positive benefits. The higher the interest rate, the less likely will the firm borrow money for new investments and vice versa. Although the interest rate is the most important factor, there are other factors which may also affect investment decisions. These include: expected inflation, expected profits, labour costs and depreciation of capital stock.

- *The higher the rate of interest the lower the level of investment.* This is especially true of residential construction. Most people purchase houses using borrowed money and interest charges represent a large proportion of the total amount paid by the consumer.

The relationship between the rate of interest, on the one hand, and investment in plant and equipment, on the other, is less clear however. Empirical studies of investment behavior suggest that short term variations in plant and equipment expenditures are not responsive to interest rate changes.

- *Expectations of future economic conditions.* If businessmen hold a pessimistic view of the future they will be reluctant to invest.

- *High demand for consumer goods:* Firms take advantage of the favourable demand conditions and invest in more capital equipment.

- *The level of profits:* If the level of profits is high, firms are able to invest more from retained profits. Retained profits are an important source of funds for investment especially when interest charges on external sources of funds are high.

Question 10

(a) Define terms of trade and explain how they are measured.

MODEL ANSWER:

A country's terms of trade is the rate at which its *goods exchange* for those of another country. This rate is measured in terms of a common currency using two index numbers namely the index of import price and the index of export price. The terms of trade are then calculated as follows:

$$\frac{\text{Index of export prices}}{\text{Index of import prices}} \times 100$$

During the *base year* the index is 100 so the terms of trade will be 100. If, during the following year, export prices rise relative to import prices the index will rise. Conversely, if export prices fall relative to import prices the index will fall.

Question 10

(b) Analyze the consequences of a change in the terms of trade.

MODEL ANSWER:

If a country's terms of trade improve, this will benefit the exporting country. The country will be able to obtain more imports for a given volume of exports. As a result national income will rise, since exports are an injection into the circular flow of income. The balance of payments in the exporting country will improve. At the same time, the countries that import these products (and have to pay higher prices for them) are worse off than previously. Their income will fall and the balance of payments will deteriorate.

It should be emphasized that the indirect effects of terms of trade improvement can be harmful, that is:

- Countries whose terms of trade have deteriorated may not be able to afford the exports from the country whose terms of trade have improved. The income of the exporting country could fall as a result.

- If the terms of trade change frequently in the domestic economy, income and employment could be unstable due to the need to make adjustments every time the terms of trade change. This may be considered undesirable for a country which wishes to stabilize income and employment.

If the country's terms of trade worsen, this will lead to deterioration in its balance of payments. It means that the country will obtain fewer imports for a given volume of exports. As a result, real national income will fall since exports are an injection into the circular flow of income. [That is, income earned from *exports* is injected into the national spending stream. In the opposite case, *imports* take money out of income flows (where *net exports* are the difference between exports and imports). When net exports are *positive*, it means an additional income to the country as equilibrium of income (Y) expands. And (Y) will fall when net exports are *negative*].

Question 11

(a) Briefly define currency depreciation and appreciation. Clearly illustrate these flows.

MODEL ANSWER:

First note that – exchange rates will fluctuate depending on the economic circumstances within and the transactions occurring between countries.

When a *currency depreciates* (i.e., decreases in price relative to another), it means, for example, that each Zambian Kwacha (ZMK) buys less foreign currency such as the Zimbabwean dollar (Zim$) than it used to, making foreign (meaning Zimbabwean or any other exporting country's) goods and services slightly more expensive to purchase. A *currency appreciates* if exactly the opposite happens. This is illustrated in **Figure 7.6** and **Figure 7.7. Figure 7.6 (a)** shows currency equilibrium market.

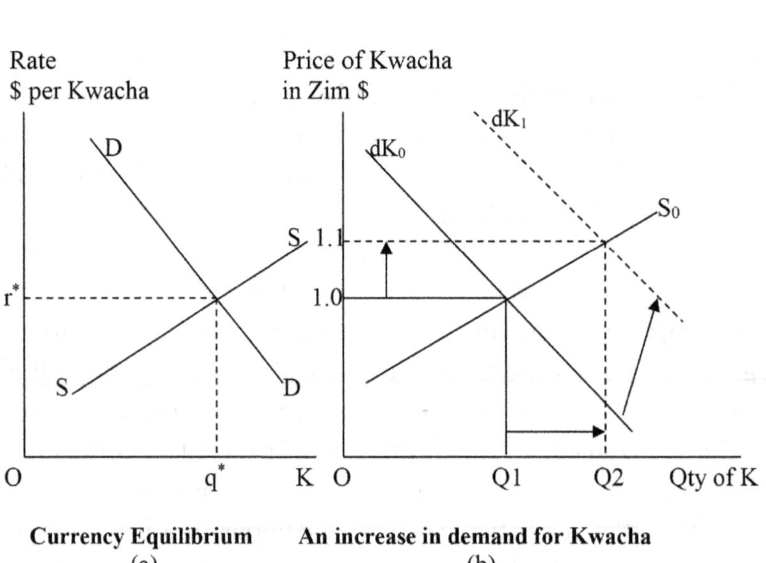

Currency Equilibrium
(a)

An increase in demand for Kwacha
(b)

As the demand for ZMKwacha (dK) shifts from dK_0 to dK_1, this does not only depict the increase in Kwacha from Q1 to Q2, but the price of Kwacha in Zimbabwean dollar (Zim$/ZMK) rises from 1.0 to 1.1. See **Figure 7.7.** Thus, the determinant of *exchange rates* could depend on the Central or Reserve Bank's decisions, such as the Bank of Zambia (BoZ) in case of Zambia or Reserve Bank in case of Zimbabwe, to supply more or less of the Kwacha or Zim-dollar currency respectively. In addition, note that domestic consumer and producer decisions regarding foreign assets, goods and services have also an impact on exchange rates.

Combining all the market forces -- the Zimbabwean supply, demand, and exchange rate per Zambian Kwacha -- they settle on *equilibrium*. In **Figure 7.6 (a)**, demand for Kwacha per day is represented by demand curve DD and supply by SS curve. The *equilibrium exchange rate* is the rate (r^*) per Kwacha and the *equilibrium quantity* of Kwacha is at (q^*) level.

For example, as productivity rises in Zambia (assumed as the domestic market in this example) making it cheaper to produce Zambian goods and services, prices falls. Hence, Zimbabweans (the foreign buyers in this case) would flock to Zambia to buy its cheaper goods and services. As Zimbabweans want more of cheaper Zambian items, the demand for Kwacha increases. This high demand for Kwacha (a tendency towards shortage) decreases the supply of Kwacha. Consequently the value of the Kwacha *appreciates.*

The *lower the prices* of a country's products, the greater the demand for them; hence, the greater the demand for that country's currency becomes (a tendency towards appreciation). These flows are illustrated in the diagrams **Figure 7.8** and **Figure 7.9** below.

Figure 7.8

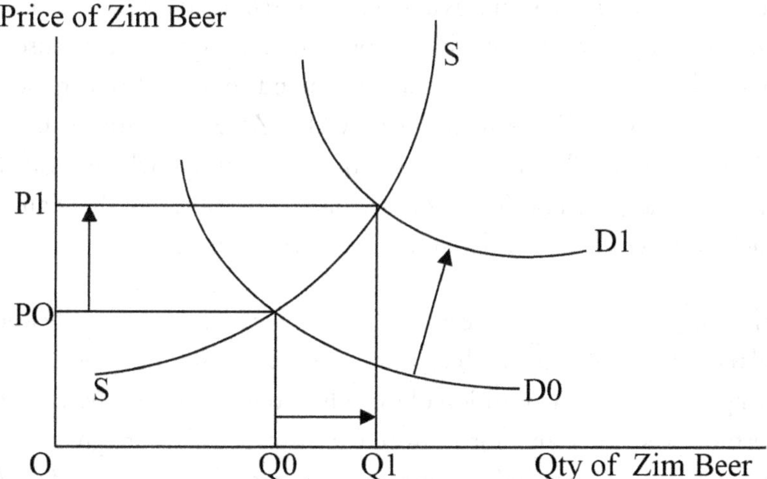

Figure 7.9

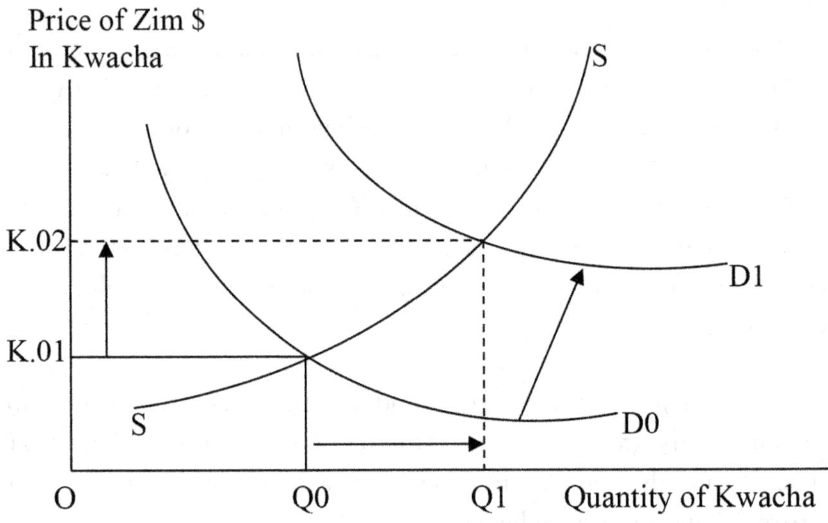

Demand for Kwacha

The two figures illustrate an example of an *increase in demand* in Zambia for Zimbabwean lager beers (in this case Zambia assumes the role of importer). As Zambians' thirst for Zimbabwean brewed beer increases, this raises the demand for Zim-dollars. As Zim-dollar demand goes up, this increases the exchange rate of the Zim$ in terms of Kwacha (ZMK). In turn, as the price of Zim$ in terms of Kwacha goes up, the Zambian Kwacha is weakened and so people purchase fewer Zim-dollars. Therefore, as the Zambian Kwacha weakens the Zim-dollar is strengthened (*appreciates*).

In the long run however, these *exchange rates fluctuations* eventually lead to a balance of trade because each country's businesses and consumers *react* by cutting down on the acquisition of the other country's expensive currency. Overtime, the back and forth switch from expensive foreign goods to cheaper domestic ones and vice versa tend to create the *balance of trade.*

Question 12

(a) Analyze the economic factors that determine a country's exchange rate.

MODEL ANSWER:

The *exchange rate* is the price of one currency in terms of another. Under a system of floating exchange rates the exchange rate is determined by the forces of supply and demand without any government interference. To gain a fuller understanding of the **determinants** of exchange rates we need to examine the factors that will cause supply and demand for currency to shift. This can be summarized as follows:

- *Differences in inflation rates*: Differences in domestic inflation rates are a major influence on the exchange rate. We can illustrate this by considering two countries -- Zimbabwe and Zambia -- that trade with each other. If there is inflation in Zambia, this will cause prices to rise in terms of the Zambian Kwacha. Zambian goods will become more expensive for Zimbabwean consumers who wish to purchase Zambian goods. Thus, the demand for Zambian Kwacha will fall. At the same time, goods from Zimbabwe will become more competitive on Zambian markets because the rate of inflation is lower. As a result, more Zimbabwean goods will be purchased by Zambians and the demand for Zimbabwean dollars will increase. The Zimbabwe dollar will appreciate relative to the Zambian Kwacha. We conclude from this analysis that an increase in the rate of inflation in Zambia will lead to a *depreciation* of the Zambian Kwacha and an *appreciation* of the Zimbabwe dollar.

- *Rate of economic growth*: Other things being equal, a country whose rate of economic growth is faster than that of its rivals will find its exports in demand. If so, the country's demand for foreign exchange will increase faster than the supply and its currency will depreciate. Exchange rates will fluctuate depending on economic circumstances and the transactions occurring within and between countries.

- *Capital movements*: Major capital movements will have an important impact on the exchange rate. They will lead to an appreciation of the currency of the capital importing country and a depreciation of the currency of the capital exporting country. These capital movements will often arise in response to interest rate differentials between countries. Other things being equal, countries with higher interest rates are able to attract more capital than those with low interest rates. For example, as foreign investments (**FI**) come in from another country, say, the United States of America, the analysis of rates follows the same principles as described for import-export transactions between countries. Zambian or Zimbabwean supply, demand, and exchange rate for the US dollar (US$) is illustrated in **Figure 7.10**.

Figure 7.10

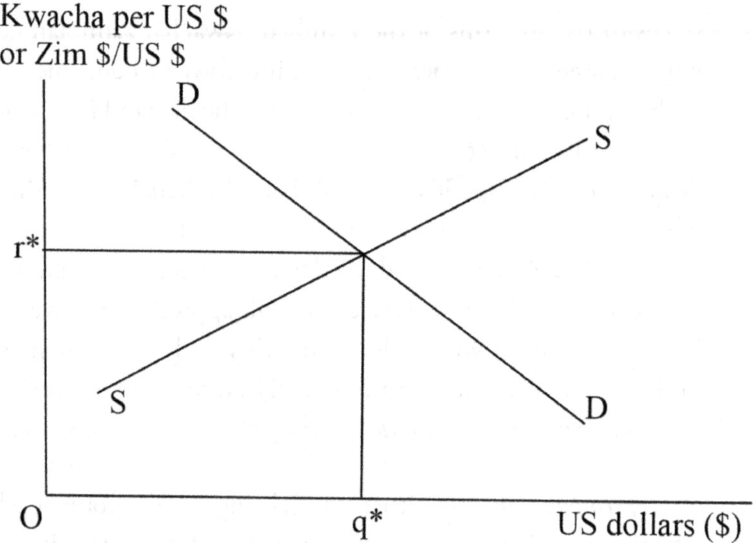

In **Figure 7.10** demand for US dollars (US$) per day is represented by DD curve and supply, the SS curve. The equilibrium *exchange rate* is r* dollars per Kwacha (ZMK) (or Zim $) as the case may be. And the *equilibrium* quantity of US dollars is given by q*.

Question 12

(b) What arguments would you advance for and against
(i) floating?
(ii) fixed exchange rates?

MODEL ANSWER:

(i) Under a system of *floating exchange rates* the currency is left to find its own level on the foreign exchange market and as such will be determined solely by supply and demand. The advantages of such a system are that, in theory at least, the balance of payments is kept automatically in equilibrium without any government interference. Thus, it is argued that under such a system the balance of payments will look after itself and policy makers can concentrate on other problems without worrying about the exchange rate. For instance, suppose that Zimbabwe has a deficit on its balance of payment with Zambia, there is thus an increased demand for Zambian Kwacha relative to the Zimbabwe dollar. The exchange rate will move in favour of Zambia.

Zimbabwean importers will have to pay more dollars to obtain the Kwacha needed to purchase Zambian goods. Providing that the demand for both imports and exports is sufficiently elastic, the balance of payments deficit will be automatically cured.

(i) A major disadvantage of *floating exchange rates* is that they increase the uncertainty associated with international trading. This arises due to two main reasons:

- The world prices of main commodities will be unstable so traders are subjected to a great deal of uncertainty on this count.
- Traders will be subjected to additional uncertainty due to fluctuations in the exchange rate.

These problems are worse if speculation is present in the market for foreign currency and commodities. If so, currency and commodity price fluctuations will be pronounced. Faced with these two problems traders will find it difficult to plan ahead.

A second consideration is that, if demand for imports and exports is inelastic, a depreciation of the currency will worsen the balance of payments disequilibrium. Furthermore, the supply of exports could be inelastic. If so, firms would find it difficult to expand supply in response to the increased demand.

(ii) A major advantage of *fixed exchange rates* is that they remove the uncertainty associated with floating exchange rates. For example, the negotiation of long term contracts and granting of long term loans or investments in other countries all become less risky under a system of fixed exchange rate in that large reserves of foreign currency may be needed to support the value of the currency. If the country is faced with a persistent deficit there is a danger that it may exhaust its reserves while trying to support the currency.

Question 13

(a) *Distinguish between absolute and comparative advantages in international trade. Illustrate your answer with examples.*

MODEL ANSWER:

Absolute advantage refers to the ability of a country or region to produce a commodity at absolutely lower cost measured in terms of factor inputs than its trading partners. For example, given one unit of resources, if country A can produce more of X but less of commodity Y than country B, total production can be increased over a situation of national self-sufficiency if A specialized in the production of X and B specialized in the production of Y.

We can illustrate the principle of absolute advantage as follows. Suppose that with one unit of resources Zimbabwe can produce 10 bags of maize or 4 tons of copper and with the same quantity of resources Zambia can produce 5 bags of maize or 12 tons of copper. Assume that initially both countries are self-sufficient with no trade but that trade eventually opens between them. Zimbabwe will specialize in the production of maize, while Zambia specialized in the production of copper. We can show that total production of both commodities will increase after trade begins.

Initially we have the following:

Table 7.2

	Copper	Maize
Zambia	12	5
Zimbabwe	4	**10**

Now assume that Zambia transfers 1 unit of resources from maize to copper production and Zimbabwe transfers one unit of resources from maize to copper. The changes in production will be as follows:

Table 7.3

	Copper	Maize
Zambia	+ 12	- 5
Zimbabwe	- 4	+ 10
Total	**8**	5

Now in terms of opportunity costs we have the following:

For copper, in Zambia 1 ton of copper costs 2 bags of maize. And in Zimbabwe, 1 bag of maize costs 1 ton of copper. Thus, in terms of opportunity costs, maize is cheaper in Zambia than in Zimbabwe and copper is cheaper in Zimbabwe than Zambia. Zimbabwe has a ***comparative advantage*** in the production of copper while Zambia has a comparative advantage in the production of maize.

Question 13

(b) What are the arguments in favour of protection?

MODEL ANSWER:
These are:

- *Infant industry argument:* Protection of young industries enables them to grow while sheltered from foreign competition. This enables them to learn by doing and exploiting economies of scale so as to enable them to compete with foreign rivals in the long run. The problem with this argument is that once some form of protection has been imposed, it may never be removed.

- *To rectify a balance of payments deficit:* A country that is persistently running in a deficit may impose controls, such as *tariffs*, to restrict the flow of imports into the country thereby creating opportunities for the growth of local industry. The problem with tariffs is that other countries may impose tariffs of their own to retaliate. End result, trade wars may ensue.

- *Revenue:* Some types of protection (such as custom duties or tariffs) yield revenue for the government.

- *Employment:* This argument says imports from low wage countries threaten the jobs of those who are in similar industries at home. Commodities imported from *low wage countries* (such as China and Mexico) are cheaper because labor costs are lower in those countries.

- *Strategic:* Some economists argue that *protection* of domestic industry is necessary to encourage production of goods that are of strategic importance. Most countries would not want to depend on foreign supplies for imports of foods, armaments as in the event of war because these supplies might be cut off.

- *To prevent dumping:* Dumping occurs when goods are sold in foreign markets at very low prices (possibly at a loss) in order to drive similar industries in other countries out of business. Consumers in the importing countries may benefit from the dumping because dumped goods are sold cheaply. If, however, the exporter is trying to obtain a monopoly position which he can exploit once he has driven out home producers, then there is a case for giving the home market some protection

- *To preserve foreign currency:* A country which imports large quantities of goods may risk depleting its foreign currency reserves. Protection is openly advocated on the grounds that it leads to savings in foreign currency.

8 Economic Policies, Economic Growth and Development

Question 1

(a) Define full employment

MODEL ANSWER:

There is no general agreement among economists as to what constitutes *full employment.* Lord Beveridge once defined it as "a situation in which there are more jobs than men." Other economists have suggested that full employment is:

- The highest level of employment compatible with stable prices. That is, full employment is thought of as a situation when the unemployment rate cannot be reduced further without accelerating inflation.

- The highest level of employment compatible with balance of payments equilibrium.

- However, most economists agree that a condition of full employment can be said to exist when the number of unfilled vacancies is equal to the number of people out of work. In such situations only a small proportion of population will be unemployed due to frictional factors.

Question 1

(b) What problems are likely to be encountered in trying to achieve full employment?

MODEL ANSWER:

In trying to achieve full employment the government is likely to face formidable problems. There are two policy options available to it, namely *fiscal policy* and *monetary policy*. Using fiscal policy, the government can reduce taxes or increase government expenditure. Both measures would help to raise the level of employment and output. Monetary policy measures involve a reduction in interest rates or relaxation on hire purchase controls.

Theoretically, it is easy for the government to establish the general direction in which monetary and fiscal variables should be altered. In practice, however, it is difficult for the government to establish the magnitude of the required change in fiscal and monetary variables that is needed to achieve a given level of employment. If the government overestimates the amount of money it should inject into the economy through expenditure to deal with a given level of unemployment, then it is likely that excess demand and inflation would result.

A related problem relates to the timing and duration of the full employment policy. Given that a certain proportion of the population is unemployed, it may not be at all clear when or for how long the full employment policy has to be pursued. The policy-maker can rely on economic forecasts but if these are inaccurate this will cause the policy to miss the mark of its target. Furthermore, a full employment policy may "suck-in" imports, especially if the country's propensity to consume imports is high. In these circumstances, if aggregate monetary demand rises, an increasing volume of imports will be purchased from abroad, thus defeating the purpose of the full employment strategy.

It is also important to consider the response of the private sector to any expansion of aggregate demand as some economists argue that increases in government expenditure have a depressing effect on private investment – the so called "*crowding out*" effect. Crowding out occurs when additional government spending displaces expenditures that in all probability would have been undertaken by the private sector.

Finally, a full employment policy that operates via monetary policy, by lowering interest rates, can result in an outflow of capital from the domestic economy. If interest rates are lower in the domestic economy relative to other countries, this makes it less profitable to invest in the domestic economy. Investors will shift funds to other countries where higher rates of interest can be obtained, thus causing balance of payments problems. In light of these many challenges, it can be concluded that implementation of a full employment policy would face many problems.

Question 1

(c) Analyze full employment in an African context.

MODEL ANSWER:

Full employment in many African countries calls for engagement with a different set of questions. In developed Western economies, eligible *labour force population* constitutes the total number of all individuals 15 years or older who can work, excluding those who are sick or institutionalized. Thus, one must be willing and able to work before he/she is part of labour statistics. In Western countries, the *labour force* then is defined as those presently employed or actively looking for work.

In many African countries, the unemployment picture is imprecise because the portion of those who are actually working or formally employed is usually small. In Zambia, for example, out of a total population of 16 million only about 400 – 600,000 are in formal employment (i.e. in economic activities related to mining or service industry). The majority of people are scrambling for survival in the informal cottage-industry sector, commercial farming, traditional agriculture, peasant farming, share cropping or simply live as villagers or rural people. Therefore a lot of people, especially youth, are in a classical sense unemployed, underemployed, and are neither looking for work nor infirm. For these people, searching for jobs is often futile because there are no jobs for the taking. Due to low economic development or lack of manufacturing industries, job creation in most African countries is either very small or disturbingly negligible.

For these reasons, it is not accurate to define the *unemployment rate* in countries like Zambia or Zimbabwe as the percentage of the labor force that is not working, but as that percentage actively seeking employment. Thus, analyzing unemployment issues in these least-developed countries (LDCs) is consequently difficult.

But for some small segments of these economies, where market forces are in play, labour market analysis is applicable in the same way that it is to Western countries that depend on supply and demand theories, using the *wage rate* as the price for labour. Note here also that the impact on the wage rate is rarely a consequence of labor unions, because their activities are more often than not political rather than economic. The analysis based on market forces is illustrated in **Figure 8.1** below.

Figure 8.1

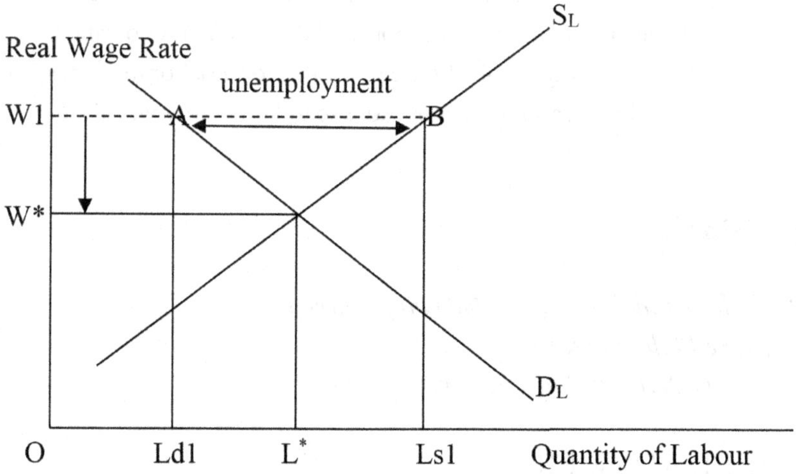

Where: $\mathbf{D_L}$ and $\mathbf{S_L}$ are the demand and supply curves for labor respectively. W1 is the real wage rate (price) in a society. At this labor price (W1), the quantity of labor demand is Ld1 and labor quantity supplied is Ls1. The difference between Ls1 and Ld1, gives the *unemployment size* at price W1.

At *labor equilibrium* (W*), the demand curve for labor ($\mathbf{D}_L$) does not shift to the right and supply curve for labor ($\mathbf{S}_L$) does not move to the left and therefore the *wage rate* remains fixed at (W*). This is plausible in a purely competitive situation.

However, in most real economic situations, the assumptions of that simplified model may not hold. Thus, clearing unemployment by forcing the wages to fall towards (W*) may not be easy because of:

- The *fallacy of composition* when we assume the behavior of one individual is faithfully representative of the group as a whole. Also what impacts one firm may not necessarily apply to others.

- Wage rigidity or the inflexibility of wages – meaning that falling wages in one industry may not necessarily contribute to the reduction in unemployment in the economy.

- And that, short run unemployment may be only a consequence of frictional and cyclical factors; which have nothing to do with the deliberate manipulation of supply and demand curves of labor. In the real world, changing of jobs, new entrants to the labor market, such as new graduates, and retirees or those abandoning jobs will always exist.

Question 2

(a) Explain and illustrate the following concepts:
(i)The Phillips curve
(ii) The Natural Rate of Unemployment

MODEL ANSWER:

(i) In 1958 A.W. Phillips established that over the period 1861-1957 there was a negative relationship between the *rate of inflation* and the *level of unemployment.* This relationship came to be known as the ***Phillips curve.***

For the policy-maker, the Phillips curve relationship had great relevance. It meant that lower levels of unemployment could only be achieved at the expense of higher rates of inflation. Diagrammatically, the Phillips curve relationship is illustrated in **Figure 8.2**.

Figure 8.2

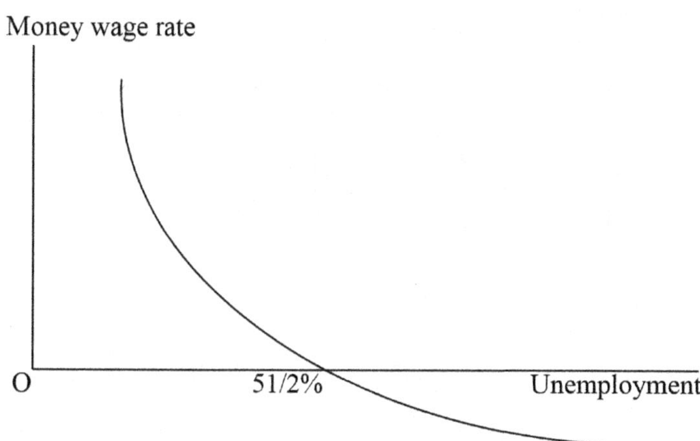

(ii) The *Natural Rate of Unemployment* hypothesis arose from the work of two monetarist economists, Milton Friedman and Edmund Phelps. Their effort helped to clarify the distinction between a long-term "core" unemployment rate and unemployment of a temporary nature. They suggested that in the short run the Phillips curve is not stable as had been thought, but that it shifts in response to changing *expectations of inflation*. Thus, higher rates of inflation lead, in the long run, to higher expected rates of inflation so that the Phillips curve keeps shifting vertically upwards. This precludes in a long-run tradeoff between unemployment and inflation. Consequently a tool known as the **NAIRU** (non-accelerating inflation rate of unemployment) became available for measuring the long-run unemployment rate.

Changes in inflationary expectations arise whenever there is divergence between *actual* and *expected rates* of inflation. For example, if the actual rate of inflation exceeds the expected rate, expectations will be revised upwards. On the other hand, if the expected rate of inflation does not exceed the actual rate, expectations of inflation will be revised downwards. Thus, for each different expected rate of inflation there is a corresponding Phillips curve. An increase in the expected rate of inflation shifts the curve upwards. A decrease shifts it downwards towards the origin. **Figures 8.3** shows a series of short-run Phillips curves that are consistent with different rates of inflation.

Figure 8.3

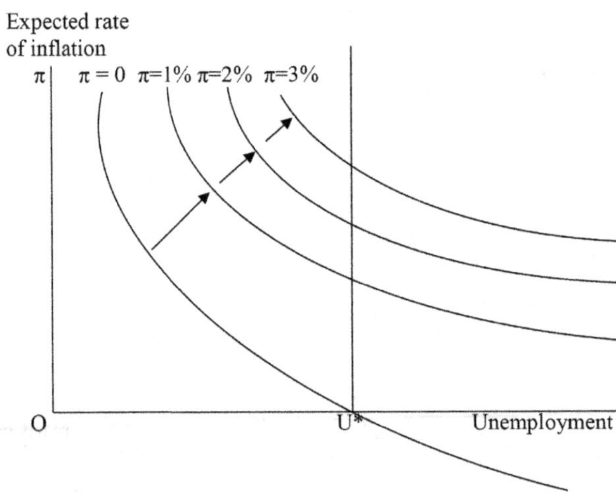

In the long run the Phillips curve is *vertical* because the rate of inflation will, over a period, be fully anticipated. The Natural Rate of Unemployment (NRU) is one that is consistent with a fully anticipated level of output. Any attempts to reduce the level of unemployment below the natural rate will result in ever increasing rates of inflation.

Question 2

(b) How can the government reduce the Natural Rate of Unemployment?

MODEL ANSWER:

The Natural Rate of Unemployment can be reduced by policies that improve the functioning of the labour market. Such policies may include the following:

- Training and retraining schemes which enable workers to acquire marketable skills.

- Measures to improve the mobility of labor, such as assistance with relocation expenses.
- Schemes designed to make it easier for workers to obtain information about job vacancies and easier for employers to obtain information about potential job applicants.
- Government assistance to firms to encourage them to locate in areas of high unemployment.
- Job sharing, that is, converting full time jobs into a large number of part-time jobs.

Question 3

(a) Define fiscal policy.

MODEL ANSWER:

Fiscal policy refers to the manipulation of government *spending* and *taxation* that is designed to steer aggregate demand in some desired direction. It is built on the premise that through a dose of government spending and/or taxation aggregate demand could be changed. In the process, other variables in the economy could also be manipulated. These are measures advanced by John Maynard Keynes who proposed that government could use these as tools for managing business cycles. Hence, they are popularly referred to as *fiscal stabilization policies* because they are used to smoothen the journey over the treacherous terrain of booms and recessions.

Question 3

(b) State specific fiscal policy tools.

MODEL ANSWER:

To stimulate or restrain economic activities, government can implement any of the following:

- Increase expenditure on infrastructure – build roads, schools, hospitals, telecommunication technology and so on.

- Make changes in taxation – such as, raise or lower personal or corporate income taxes; introduce sales or excise taxes; introduce tax incentives for new investments; introduce tax credits or remove tax exemptions.

All these measures work through the supply and demand of goods and services in an economy.

Question 3

(c) Outline the objectives of fiscal policy.

MODEL ANSWER:
The main objectives of fiscal policy are as follows:

- To maintain a high level of employment and economic activity;

- To minimize fluctuations in employment and output;

- To control inflation;

- To achieve an equitable distribution of income and wealth;

- To promote economic growth.

Fiscal policy impacts are felt through what is known as the *Keynesian multiplier* (**k**). This multiplier (**k**) equals 1/(1-**MPC**) or the ratio between the changes in income and the change in investment (ΔY/ΔI), where **MPC** is marginal propensity to consume. Details of the **k** multiplier are not discussed here.

Question 3

(d) Analyze how fiscal policy works with particular reference to:
i) Expansionary measures.
ii) Contractionary fiscal policy.

MODEL ANSWER:

Through expenditure and its power of taxation and borrowing, government can either stimulate or restrain economic activities.

- *Expansionary measures:*

During a recession, the aggregate demand is too low and usually the unemployment rate is high. And typically, the economic growth (output) is negative or too small. To reverse this trend the government adopts *expansionary fiscal policy,* implying either increasing government spending and/or introducing some tax cuts or incentives. This is illustrated in **Figure 8.4.**

Figure 8.4

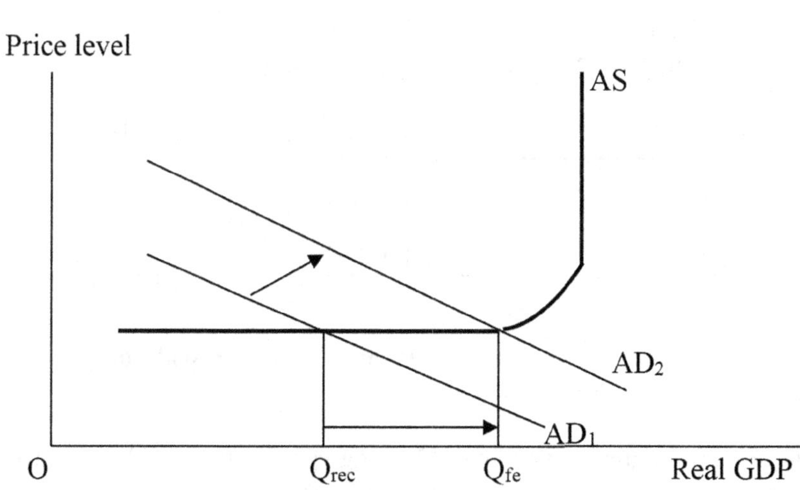

Expansionary Fiscal Policy

Where aggregate demand (**AD**) shifts right from AD_1 to AD_2 – increasing real GDP output from recession quantity (Qrec) towards full employment output at (Qfe) -- the Aggregate supply (AS) at some point becomes vertical (i.e. remains constant).

NOTE: As long as equilibrium remains below full employment, in general, the price level holds steady.

- *Contractionary fiscal policy*:

On the other hand if the economy is experiencing *high inflation* – aggregate demand (AD) may be too high and economic growth may be red hot with high levels of employment -- to cool off things, the government could use contractionary fiscal policy such as reduced spending and/or tax increases. See **Figure 8.5** for illustration.

Figure 8.5

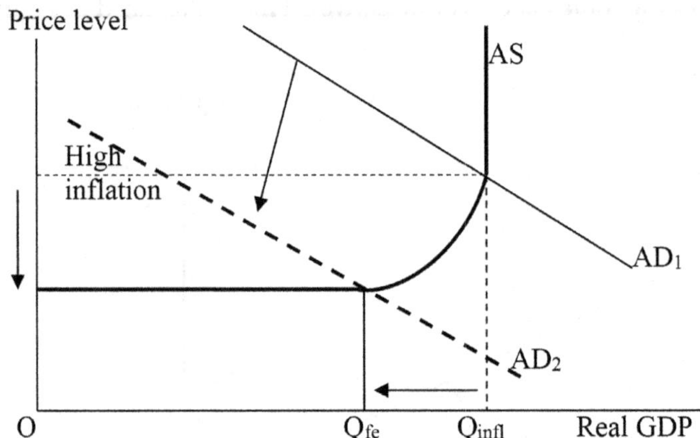

Contractionary Fiscal Policy

Where AS = aggregate supply; AD = aggregate demand; Qfe = output at full employment; Q_{infl} = output with inflation, the government, by decreasing disposable income through, say, tax increases together with reduced spending, the government could shift aggregate demand (AD) left (or down) from AD1 to AD2; which in turn could lead to a decrease in the inflation rate. Note also, that as you shift from high inflation level towards full employment, real GDP drops.

Question 4

(a) Define monetary policy

MODEL ANSWER:

Just like and in addition to fiscal policy, monetary policy measures are used to contend with an economy which is either in a period of *recession or high inflation.* During a *recession,* interest rates are lowered to increase money supply growth. Commercial banks get more money for lending and they could lower interest rates to encourage borrowers to access money for buying, say, houses, cars or other consumer durables. Businesses also borrow more to supply goods and services. Hence, increased spending by both consumers and producers expands output leading to the elimination (or decline) of recession. This is the easy money policy.

When there is *high inflation,* a tight monetary policy is the appropriate tool to use. This means, in other words, raising of interest rates and the reduction of the rate of money supply growth. Higher interest rates discourage spending by households and reduce investments by suppliers. Hence, total aggregate demand falls thereby reducing high inflation.

Question 4

(b) Illustrate how monetary policy works.

MODEL ANSWER:

(i) During a *recession* – the Central Bank, such as the Bank of Zambia (BoZ) or Zimbabwe's Reserve Bank, uses its powers to adopt an easy money policy by *lowering interest rates* and increases money supply growth. This is illustrated in **Figure 8.6.**

Figure 8.6

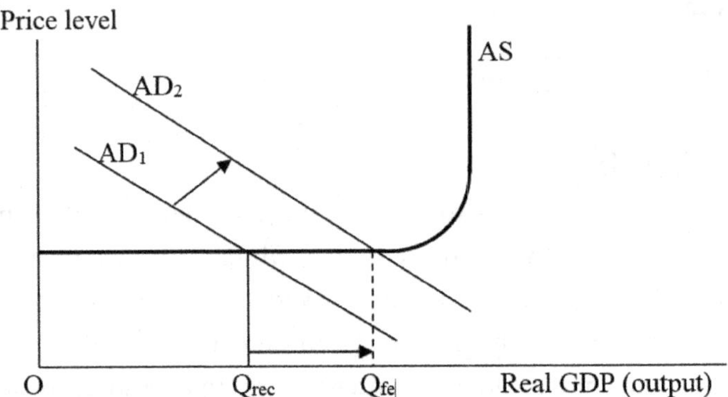

Where AS = aggregate supply; AD = aggregate demand; Q_{rec} = output during recession; and Q_{fe} = output at full employment:

As interest rates are lowered, first, this helps commercial banks and other financial institutions to build their financial resources. In turn, these banks lower their interest rates inducing more borrowing by people. As consumers have easy access to loans, they make more purchases of big items like houses and vehicles. More borrowing by both consumers and firms increases the money supply, which in turn increases output needed in the economy. It is the spending of households and businesses which pushes aggregate demand (AD) *outward* from AD_1 to AD_2. As this happens, *recession* is eliminated and *full employment* shifts towards equilibrium (Qfe). Real GDP also increases as illustrated in **Figure 8.6.**

(ii) With *high inflation* in the economy, central banks or reserve banks adopt a *tight monetary policy* usually applied together with lower government spending and taxes increase to reduce high inflation. This is illustrated in **Figure 8.7.**

Figure 8.7

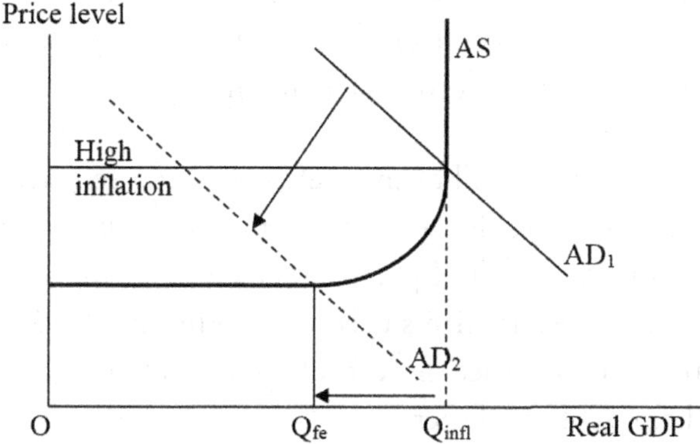

Where AS = aggregate supply; AD = aggregate demand; Qfe = output at full employment; Q_{infl} = output with inflation:

Tightening of the money supply lowers money reserve levels even at commercial banks, limiting the amount of money available for lending out, apply higher interest rates. These high interest rates dampen borrowing. But as households and businesses borrow less; the money supply is decreased, which lowers spending. It is this decreased spending by firms and consumers which shifts aggregate demand (AD) *backward (left)* from AD_1 to AD_2 ending the *high inflation.*

Question 5

(a) Discuss the relative efficiency of fiscal and monetary policy.

MODEL ANSWER:

Monetary and fiscal policies are not mutually exclusive but complementary. Even so, economists disagree about their relative effectiveness. The main areas of disagreement are summarized below.

- *Lags in the effect of monetary policy:* Delays in data collection and processing and in the process of decision making can result in lags in the effect of this policy. These delays have important implications for the relative effectiveness of the two policy instruments. For example, using fiscal policy, the government can influence the level of aggregate demand and hence income or it can use monetary policy to influence interest rates and hence investment and income.

In this case, fiscal policy will be more effective because it acts directly on the choice variables, that is, consumption, investment and government spending. Lags in the effect of policy are likely to be much longer in the case of investment because firms need time to install additional capacity. If the objective is to influence the level of investment, monetary policy will be superior because it acts faster.

Another consideration is *decision lags,* that is, the time it takes for policy makers to consider, adopt and then implement the policy. Decisions to change the money supply or interest rates can be taken more quickly by the Reserve (or Central) Bank than decisions to alter government spending or the level of taxes. Recall that fiscal variables are normally altered only once a year at budget time.

* *Crowding out:* Monetarists suggest that fiscal policy will be less effective than monetary policy because of crowding out effects. Some ways of financing government expenditure have secondary effects on the economy so that the net effects on aggregate demand and the level of income are negligible. The exact nature of crowding out effects will depend on the method chosen by the government to finance the expenditure. For instance, assume that the government increases the level of taxation, this will cause a reduction in disposable income and consumers will cut spending on goods and services. Therefore, the main crowding out effect in this case is the reduction in consumption expenditure.

Alternatively, assume that the increased government expenditure is financed by issuing bonds to the public, i.e. borrowing. This will result in greater competition for funds on the money and capital markets. Interest rates will increase which will displace interest-sensitive private expenditures.

Finally, if the extra government spending is financed by printing money, this will according to monetarists, not have any crowding out effects and the net effect will be expansionary. Therefore monetary policy is considered to be more effective.

* *Interest rate elasticity of demand for money:* **Keynesian Economists** argue that investment is inelastic with respect to the interest rate, making monetary policy relatively weak. On the opposite end of scale are the **monetarists** who suggest that investment is elastic with respect to the rate of interest so that monetary policy will have a powerful effect on the level of income.

* *Government debts:* Fiscal policy results in an increase in the size of the government debt. Monetary policy does not directly give rise to an increase in the size of the government debt.

* *Wider objectives:* Monetary policy works primarily via changes in interest rates and the money supply. Fiscal policy is more pervasive and can be used to achieve a wider range of objectives, such as the achievement of an equitable distribution of income or a better balance in the level of employment between different regions of the country.

Question 6

(a) Define labor mobility.

MODEL ANSWER:

Labor mobility refers to the ability of labor to move from one region to another or from one occupation to another in response to changing economic conditions. The movement of labor from one region to another is termed geographical mobility, while the movement of labor from one occupation to another is known as occupational mobility.

Question 6

(b) What are the main barriers to labor mobility? Illustrate your answer with examples.

MODEL ANSWER:

The principle reasons for ***geographical immobility*** of labor are as follows:

* *Expense:* It is expensive to move a family together with its possessions to another area. There may also be additional expenses involved in buying and selling houses or there may be accommodation shortages in the area where the worker wants to move. For example, in Zimbabwe or Zambia, the level of poverty in the rural areas is such that many people would not be able to afford the rent in the urban areas should they move to look for jobs. Job seekers often have to rely on the generosity of relatives or friends until they find employment. In recent years, accommodation shortages in the main urban centers have also been acute.

* *Social ties:* Moving to another area often entails leaving one's friends, relatives, clubs, churches, and so on. The individual who wants to move to another area may be deterred by the fact that it may take a long time for him to establish similar relationships in the new area.

* *Job opportunities:* Workers may be ignorant about job opportunities and wage levels in the other areas. In Zimbabwe or Zambia many people, particularly in the rural areas, do not read newspaper and are unlikely to be aware of the job opportunities in the cities.

Occupational barriers to labor mobility arise for many reasons.

* *Natural Ability:* People differ in natural ability and some occupations require a high level of intelligence and particular natural aptitudes. The lack of these attributes may prevent some people from taking up certain jobs.

* *Education and training:* Some jobs require long periods of training and a high level of education. However, for people nearing retirement age, it may not be worth their while to undertake additional training. Trade unions and other professional associations may make entry into certain occupations difficult or workers may be ignorant about opportunities in other areas.

Question 6

(c) How can the government increase the domestic mobility of labor?

MODEL ANSWER:

Greater labor mobility can be achieved by attacking the causes of **labor immobility**. Some of the measures to improve labor mobility could include assistance with moving expenses, that is "taking workers to work" or offer firms financial assistance to encourage them to move to areas of high unemployment. Thus, the Zimbabwe or Zambian governments actively encourage investment in rural projects where there is a large pool of unemployed people.

Other measures to improve *geographical mobility* could involve improving the flow of information, that is, by making more information available to workers about opportunities in other areas or regions.

The government could also make it easier for people to enter certain occupations. This can be achieved by making available more information on opportunities in other occupations. The government could also use its power to influence trade unions and other professional organizations to modify their regulations regarding the length of apprenticeship periods and the number of candidates who are admitted to apprenticeships each year. It could also provide incentives or set up training and retraining facilities for workers who require new skills.

Question 7

(a) Describe the different types of unemployment.

MODEL ANSWER:

There are **four** main types of unemployment namely, seasonal, frictional, structural and cyclical.

* *Seasonal Unemployment:* This arises due to the seasonal nature of certain types of economic activities. In many countries the climate cycle gives rise to seasonal unemployment. Examples are to be found in the farming, fishing, tourist and construction industries where the demand for labour tends to increase sharply during the peak season and decline during the off-peak season.

* *Frictional:* This arises due to ignorance about available job opportunities and due to labor immobility. People change jobs or may be unemployed for all sorts of reasons. If they change jobs it can take some time for them to find new ones. This is the transitional and short-run frictional unemployment rate. And because workers want to switch jobs voluntarily, its solution lies in free exchange of information.

* *Structural:* This type of unemployment arises from labor immobility brought about by long term changes in the conditions of supply and demand. Given geographical disparities, structural changes within industries and between industries coupled with changing demand patterns and technology could render some workers temporarily unemployable because they do not possess the skills suitable for the vacant jobs. Thus we get an occupational mismatch between the jobs available and the skills of the unemployed.

* *Cyclical:* Cyclical unemployment is associated with the trade cycle and is sometimes referred to as deficient demand unemployment. It arises due to inadequate aggregate demand. Thus, it is a short-run problem caused by economic fluctuations, such as reductions in

aggregate or total demand for goods and services. When for example, production activities in the economy falls, fewer jobs are created causing unemployment to rise.

Question 7

(b) How can the government tackle the level of unemployment?

MODEL ANSWER:

A government seeking to reduce the level of unemployment can use monetary and fiscal policies.

Using **fiscal policy,** the government can influence the level of consumption or investment by changing taxes or government expenditure. For example, a reduction in corporate tax would leave firms with more funds to plough back into their businesses and so stimulate investment. A move from direct to indirect taxation would increase consumption because it would transfer purchasing power to poorer people who have a higher marginal propensity to consume.

More generally, reductions in taxation will increase disposable income and, providing that this is not saved, total spending in the economy will increase.

The government can also increase its own spending in goods and services. Since government expenditure is an injection into the circular flow of income this will increase output and employment.

Using **monetary policy**, the government can influence the cost and availability of credit. Reductions in interest rates make it cheaper for firms to borrow. This will in turn stimulate controls to influence the cost and availability of credit. Banks can be requested to be selective in their lending policies for example, by asking them to grant loans for investment that generates jobs while at the same time discouraging loans on investment that does not create employment.

Monetary policy is also concerned with controls of hire purchase agreements on durable goods such as cars, furniture and television sets. Relaxing hire purchase terms will make funds more easily available to consumers which will indirectly influence spending. Production and employment in the durable goods sector will increase as a result.

Question 8

(a) *What are the main causes of underdevelopment? Illustrate your answer with reference to Zimbabwe or Zambia.*

MODEL ANSWER:

The **main causes** of underdevelopment are as follows:

- *Lack of natural resources:* Countries with large quantities of natural resource deposits find it relatively easier to develop than those who are poorly endowed. For instance, a number of oil rich countries such as Libya, Saudi Arabia and Kuwait have large per capita incomes. Both Zimbabwe and Zambia have large amounts of fertile agricultural land, mineral resources, and forests, all of which are important elements in determining the rate of economic growth in these countries.

- *Inefficiency in the use of resources:* Inefficiency in the use of resources may arise for many reasons such as low technical knowhow, lack of skills, rigid habits and customs, illiteracy and poor health, poor work ethics, or due to corruption or nepotism at the work place. It may also arise because of poor policies which cause people to produce the wrong products or prevent companies from making full use of available resources. In terms of the production possibility curve, inefficiency in the use of resources puts the economy in question inside the production possibility curve at a point such as E in **Figure 8.8**.

Figure 8.8

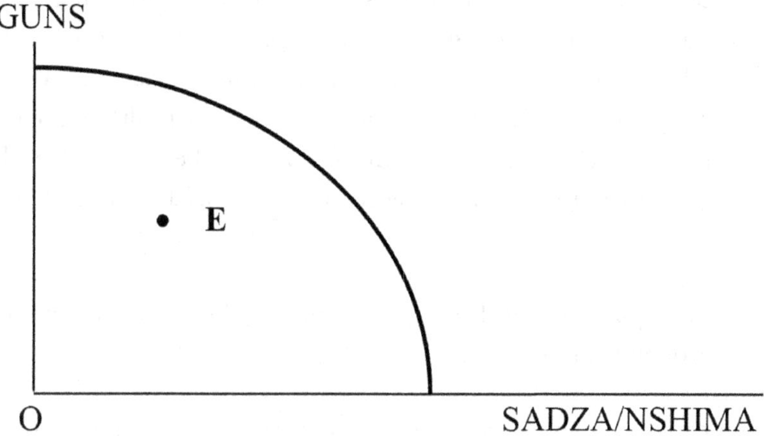

* *Infrastructures:* Good transport and communication systems are important for the swift delivery of goods and information. As far as several African countries are concerned, this is an important consideration. For a completely land-locked Zambia, the opening of (Tazara) Tanzania Zambia Railway line, Kapiri Mposhi to Dar-es Salaam was a great relief.

In case of Zimbabwe, problems could potentially arise in trying to transport goods through a hostile South Africa, especially if full force sanctions against that country remain in place. In recent years we saw that political dissidents have been responsible for disrupting the railway line through Mozambique on a number of occasions. Problems of this nature may seriously affect a country's future growth prospects.

- *Inadequate human resources:* It is important for a country to not only have a large labor force but one that is appropriately and well trained. Countries need the particular skills of professionals such as engineers, scientists, economists, accountants, and so on. As far as the total amount of labor goes, both Zambia and Zimbabwe have abundant quantities of unskilled labor though there are shortages of particular skills. Such shortages have sometimes been alleviated by employment of expatriate staff or nationals from neighboring countries. However, foreign workers or nationals from neighboring countries are only a short term solution to the problem and may cause a drain on foreign currency, especially if a portion of their salary is paid in foreign currency as is usually the case. Another dimension of this development necessity is the health of the labor force. An unhealthy labor force is bound to be less efficient than one which is healthy. This accentuates the need for a good health system.

- *Inadequate capital:* Both foreign and local capital is required for economic growth.

Foreign capital allows the country to purchase imports that are required in the process of production and may take the form of private investment or aid and grants from other countries or international organizations as well as from export earnings.

Local sources of capital come from people's savings. Thus it is essential to have sound financial institutions which provide a wide range of savings facilities for investors such as commercial banks, building societies and merchant banks. Zimbabwe is fortunate in having one of the most well developed financial systems in the whole of Africa which caters for the needs of different investors. Zambia has since tried to catch up.

- *Education:* An uneducated, illiterate labor force is likely to be less efficient than one which is educated. The governments of Zimbabwe and Zambia have been very active in this area. Since independence this sector has expanded phenomenally and now uses up approximately 27% and 37% of their countries' respective annual budgets. The benefits of an educated populace take time to be realized but the present expansion in education should have a favourable impact on future economic growth in both countries.

Question 9

(a) Define gross domestic product (GDP)

MODEL ANSWER:

Gross Domestic Product (GDP) is a measure of a country's output or the economic growth of a country. It is expressed as the total market value of all final goods and services produced in a country for one year. GDP is therefore computed by either *adding up* everything that is spent on final goods and services (the expenditure method), or *adding up* all the income that is earned by the different factors of production, such as: rent, wages, interest, and profit in producing final goods and services (the income method). The two GDPs, which are final values, should be equal, as expenditure for one individual is an income for another.

Although GDP is a more common method of measuring output, Gross National Product (GNP) is another concept by which a country's economic level is described. The GNP is the *total value* of all final goods and services a country produces from all the factors of production it owns.

Since GDP is calculated based on *market prices* when goods are sold, to allow for changes in the level of prices from year to year, it is adjusted to get *real GDP* (a constant dollar GDP). The unadjusted GDP is *nominal* (or current-dollar GDP). The change in GDP shows how much a country's economy has expanded from one year to the next. This is usually expressed in percentage terms.

Thus, calculation of real GDP growth rate is: -

$$\text{Is} = \frac{(\text{real gdp yr 2- real gdp yr 1})}{(\text{real gdp yr 1})} \times 100$$

Comparison of the standards of living between different countries is done by comparing, on a per capita basis, figures of GDP values calculated using the income approach. A real per capita GDP is the total amount of income earned by a country divided by its total population. Citizens from countries with high per capita real GDP are presumably judged to be better off (i.e., have a higher standard of living) than those with lower GDPs.

The calculation of total GDP using expenditure approach is as follows:

$$\text{GDP (or Y)} = C + G + I + (X - M)$$

Where: C = Personal households consumption expenditure
G = Government purchases
I = Gross private investments
(X – M) = Net exports; (X = exports; M = imports).

Question 10

(a) What are the main sources of economic growth?

MODEL ANSWER:

Unless a country has sustainable economic growth, it is unlikely to achieve high living standards. Economic growth refers to an increase in the country's **GNP** (gross national product). If, for example, the level of GNP in year 1 is $100 and this increases to $106 in year 2, then the rate of growth over the two years is 6%. For this rate to be meaningful it has to be measured over periods where the rate of capacity utilization was roughly similar. The main sources of economic growth are as follows:

* *Quality and quantity of capital:* The size of the country's capital stock and its quality are important determinants of its economic growth rate.

* *Innovation:* New knowledge helps to improve the efficiency with which resources are utilized and this will in turn lead to higher rates of growth.

* *Quality of Human Capital:* The skills of the labour force, its education and health will be important determinants of economic growth. A skilled, educated and healthy labour force is likely to be more efficient in performing its tasks. The higher rate of productivity of the labour force will in turn generate higher rates of growth. Thus, firms carefully watch labour costs per unit.

* *Size of the population:* Population provides the labor resources necessary for development, therefore the size of the population will be an important determinant of growth. This point needs to be qualified by noting that the size of the population can be a hindrance as well as a source of growth. Too large a population can make it difficult for the government to provide jobs for all the citizens who require one. There must obviously be some optimum population which, when combined with the nation's capital stock, will result in the maximum output per head. Also, if the population has a sizeable proportion of unproductive members, such as the old, those too young and the infirm, these individuals will not be able to contribute much to economic growth.

* *Social and legal institutions:* Social habits or cultural factors also affect economic growth. For example, it has been suggested that certain religious patterns are more conducive to economic growth than others, while in other societies the pattern of land ownership makes it difficult to utilize modern production methods and achieve economies of scale. Economic development tends to be *conducive* in societies where charter of rights and property rights are developed, together with both an efficient and impartial judicial system.

* *Entrepreneurship and knowledge:* These are also important factors of production. Entrepreneurship is the ability to organize economic activities, assume risks, and achieve effective results. Usually the firm

owner, manager, or investor oversees the efficient use of land, raw materials, labor and capital.

Question 10

(b) What is the role of government in the economy?

MODEL ANSWER:

Instead of considering only the behavior of firms and households in the economy, government tries to look at the economy as a whole (the macro-economic perspective) to see how things can be improved to reach equilibrium or full employment for the whole society. There are some governments who believe in the *laissez-faire doctrine.* Using this approach, governments rely on natural laws to regulate economic activities instead of relying on various taxes and regulations.

This doctrine can be traced back to Adam Smith who argued that since human beings are motivated by *self-interest* or *profit*, these factors or incentives would make people work together to advance the common good. The premise here is that the desire to better one's condition in life leads a society to advanced economic development.

But in most societies today, the political and ideological orientation of the specific country will determine the level of involvement of government in the economy. Those using the *model of capitalism*, like America (USA), tend to prefer less government involvement in the economy and reduced taxes for both firms and households. In capitalist countries, private firms feature more prominently in the economy.

Then there are those like the Scandinavian countries and Canada, whose economies resemble "welfare states". They promote substantial government support for their citizens (financed through high corporate taxes) to ensure economic stability and a fair distribution of wealth. During periods of unemployment, workers receive some form of assistance (like relief programmes, social assistance, or unemployment insurance) from the national government.

Choosing an entirely different path, there are those countries that have adopted *socialist* and *communist models of development*. Prominent among those countries are Russia and the Peoples' Republic of China. In these countries, not only do corporate or income taxes tend to be high but government's involvement in economic activities is quite high. The role of the market and private industry is limited. Dependency on government hand-outs and social programmes tend to undermine personal initiative and rein in the incentive for self-betterment.

Question 10

(c) How might the government increase the rate of economic growth?

MODEL ANSWER:

There are a number of policies which the government can adopt to increase the rate of economic growth in the economy as a whole. Such policies usually work by shifting resources from current consumption towards increased capacity to produce goods and services. Or the government could transfer resources from unprofitable and dying industries to those with substantial growth potential.

The government could increase the level of investment through deliberate policies designed to keep interest rates low. However, such policies may result in increased consumer spending rather than investment. Thus, it may be more effective for the government to act on business incentives, for example, by reducing tax rates.

To encourage innovation the government could provide research grants to universities, research institutes and companies or undertake joint research ventures with the private sector.

The government could also increase its own spending on education and training. This would provide a pool of well-educated people with the expertise to undertake complex tasks to facilitate economic development.

Question 11

(a) Discuss the role of public policy and economic model for development.

MODEL ANSWER:

Income or earnings is paid to the factors of production - labor, land, and capital -- for their involvement in the production process. Labor is paid *wages*, landowners obtain *rent*, and owners of capital get *profits*. In a market economy, it is assumed that the distribution of income between different factors of production is done fairly through competitive forces in the market place; as opposed to a socialist or communist model where it is argued that resource allocation is done through cumbersome and inefficient bureaucratic processes. But in reality, sometimes this market-place assumption does not hold true (in the sense that fair distribution is not achieved). Even in a market system, a society may sometimes devise other ways of leveling out income. Among the options available, public policy may be one such method to limit or reduce inequality. This is where the discussion on levies and taxes, such as windfall tax and royalties, become relevant.

Depending on the type of resources one owns and the prices they command, a discussion may ensue to arrive at some fair point of income distribution to all parties. Each party hopes to maximize its share of benefits. Capital owners talk of disincentives to invest if they are not satisfied with the level of returns or the size of their profits. As leverage, they also argue that they deserve comparable returns as in capitalist and fully functional market systems where owners of land and other natural resources get rewarded handsomely. Since major institutional sources of capital and finance, like the World Bank and IMF, are usually on the investors' side, undue influence or pressure is exerted on policy makers in less-developed-countries (LDCs). This restricts the income shares these countries can earn from their resources thereby indirectly worsening poverty.

Consider mineral resources owned by Zambia for example. Foreign investors bring in capital to develop these rich mineral deposits like copper or uranium. It is important that the two sides engage in formal discussions, (validated by policy instruments and agreements), which would lead to a fairer distribution of income between the two sides resulting from the process of extracting and selling those minerals. That is, the share of income going to the investors must not be unreasonably high (so called excessive profits) as compared to tax revenues accruing to the Zambian State.

Allowing capital owners to take home a larger share from mineral earning is really a transfer of wealth from poor Zambia to richer developed countries. This worsens the inequality paradigm between the poor South and richer North (providing capital and management) or between the emerging markets and the rising economic "Asian Tigers" (basically China and India) who are the major consumers of these resources. This suggests that, if nothing is done about this scenario, less income flowing to raw materials owners will ensure that the people in these countries become poorer and poorer.

Question 12

(a) Distinguish between capital and income.

MODEL ANSWER:

Capital is a man-made resource that is used in the production of more wealth. *Income* is defined as any addition to the existing capital stock. Thus, both capital and income are a form of wealth but whereas income is a flow, capital is a stock.

Economists distinguish between different types of capital. *Fixed capital* refers to the assets and capital investments that are used in the production process, such as stocks of heavy equipment, raw materials and semi-finished goods. *Human capital* refers to the physical talents and skills as well as the mental capabilities possessed by the citizens of a country. Such skills can be acquired through education or training.

Question 12

(b) What is the economic significance of capital?

MODEL ANSWER:

Capital is very important in the economy. It makes possible the production of more goods and services for consumption, thus raising the standard of living of the citizens of the country.

As more production is undertaken, the level of employment will increase (since more jobs are provided to increase output). This makes it possible for yet greater production. If the capital stock is increasing, a greater level of production can be undertaken thus raising the rate of economic growth. A higher rate of economic growth makes it possible for the country to redistribute resources more evenly. In the process, overall poverty is reduced.

Finally, an increase in the nation's capital stock means that other factors of production can be released to undertake other tasks, thus enabling a higher volume of production to be undertaken. It also makes it possible for the citizens of the country to reduce the number of hours spent on work and thus enjoy more leisure. Thus the size of the country's capital stock is very important to and for the national economy.

9 The Last Word

As we come to the end of this book, we are sure that readers will appreciate the usability, appeal and relevance of the subject matter and the materials covered. We hope that those who will be interested in reading it will be avail the opportunity to seek deeper knowledge about economics.

We believe that our strong niche audience of students preparing for their A-levels, particularly those in Sub-Saharan African countries, will benefit from this project.

Other readers interested in learning about the basic economics foundations, will also find the text informative and approachable. No doubt that adds value to the book's usability and appeals.

Also, looking at current global affairs – that is, what is in the public square, are themes discussed in this book.

Take for example the debate around the concept of *free-trade* between two or more groups of countries – North American Free Trade Agreement (NAFTA) as a typical case, was covered in Chapter 7. NAFTA is a trade agreement signed in (1994) between the USA, Canada and Mexico to allow free flow of goods and services between these countries without hindrance.

Tariff barriers were removed between these three countries. The opposite of free-trade is *protectionism* (anti-competition), whose objective is realized through the introduction of government *regulations* and *tariffs*.

The emergence of Donald Trump as president of the United States of America has triggered a heated debate about free-trade. Trump has complained, Supported by farm lobby and his political base, Donald Trump has complained that *Mexico's cheap labor* and the *Canadian Supply Management* have worked against the United States.

Supply Management is a scheme put in place to protect Canadian eggs, poultry and dairy industries. Trump argues that this is a form of protectionism as production quotas, subsidies and price regulation shield Canadian producers. Indeed, we have argued in this book that tariffs, quotas to limit production to drive price up, discourage foreign competition.

Further, Americans argue that as Canadian government controls dairy products imports, this does not only encourage state-sanctioned cartels in this industry but also tends to minimize the role of the market. In the process, as the shortage of demand for the American dairy produce is constrained, there is a tendency for oversupply.

To level the playing field, supposedly in the name of fair-trade, the United States has decided to impose a twenty-five percent (25%) tariffs on Canadian Steel and Aluminum. In response, Canada has introduced a retaliatory tariff measure. In the end, the impact of the American tariffs which have been extended to other European Union (EU) countries and China has provoked a trade war.

This is not useful in the already interconnected free-markets of the world. In Chapter 7, we discussed that due to *comparative advantage* reasons, international trade could not be avoided. A case can be made that some countries, economies or productive systems have the capacity to do certain things *better*, *cheaper*, or *faster* than competitors. This fact cannot be ignored, even by powerful economies like the United States.

It was argued in the text that Zambia has got a comparative advantage in the production of copper than Zimbabwe; while Zimbabwe is better placed in the production of maize and tobacco.

Another theoretical underpinning covered in this book, which can be illustrated with a real-life example is *Monetary Policy*. In July 2018, the Bank of Canada (BoC) raised overnight rate target to one-and-half ($1^{1}{}_{/2}$) percent. As a result, the Bank rate was correspondingly raised to one-and-three-quarters ($1^{3}{}_{/4}$) percent and deposit rate was one-and-a-quarter ($1^{1}{}_{/4}$) percent.

Similarly, the Central Banks in Zambia and Zimbabwe can perform the same functions to control their monetary policies. Taking note that – higher interest rates dampen household spending, which in turn works its way into the economy. For example, increasing costs of loans for mortgages, cars, or student loans.

For resource-rich countries like Canada, Zambia, and Zimbabwe, –higher commodity prices in the market, boost their economic growths as a result of earnings from export.

Zambia and Zimbabwe are both members of the Southern Africa Development Countries (SADC) – a region so endowed with abundant natural resources among which are: copper, cobalt, gold, uranium, diamonds and arable land. An average person survives on less than two dollars ($2.00) per day. If economic development can be boosted, the per-capita [US$1178.4 (2016)] for Zambia, and [US$1008.6 (2016)] for Zimbabwe increased, it could lead to increase in living standard of the people.

Currently, exploitation of these countries' natural resources is below optimal. If economic activities could be expanded and diversified, in the Common Market for Eastern and Southern Africa (COMESA) comprising of 19 countries, which is the biggest regional economic organization in Africa with a population of 390 million people, benefits accruing to its citizens could perhaps be increased ten-fold.

In much of this book, we have tried to explain how economics and its theories affect everyone. Demonstrating amply how individual households and firms – both large and small companies, make decisions such that they end up creating wealth beneficial to themselves. The discussion, of course also included those decisions which lead to 'undesired' outcomes.

Using *Model Answers*, we could, for example, show how and why the government pays more attention to *public goods* such as bridges, schools and hospitals than *private goods* such as cars and TV sets. We explained the relevancy and necessity of public goods fully.

In the section dealing with supply and demand matrix of Goods and Services (G & S) – we tried to tie economics to the global context. We analyzed the impacts of household and firm decisions on the resource use and the environment. What happens for example, in the long-run when finite natural resources are used up? Does that signal the end of human civilization?

In chapter 1 we learn that scarcity breeds new technologies. The use and application of natural copper could as time passes, be replaced by copper alloys or other materials. Even real diamonds could potentially be replaced by artificial ones. This admittedly a puzzle to a layman is clearly explained in economics – as the impacts of *price* and/or *substitution effects*, and changes in *preferences*.

We also discovered that as technology advances, even *human labor* could be replaced by *capital goods*. Machinery (capital goods) in the assembly lines in factories, can easily replace manual labor. As technology has allowed us to produce more, productivity improved tremendously. Our lives have simultaneously improved, leading in some cases beyond prosperity and well-being but even to decadence.

While economics has the power to explain these improvements, and self-sufficiency, which make life easier, it is still however blunt in analyzing ethical and moral issues. Questions such as: would there be anything wrong to consume Genetically Modified Foods (GMOs) or artificially produced foods, so-called Franken Foods rather than organic or naturally grown foods? To what extent can we depend on animal and plant breeding? Why is half of the world's population still living in poverty when tons of food is being thrown away?

Economic theories would never produce satisfactory answers to these questions. For challenges like re-distribution and other technically complex issues, is where interdisciplinary analysis becomes useful.

REFERENCES

Bolotta, Angelo, Don Mills, 2002. *Economics Now: analyzing current issues.* Toronto, ON: Oxford university Press.

Cleaver, Tony, 2011. *Economics: the basics,* 2nd ed., New York: Routledge.

Farnham, Paul G., 2010. *Economics for Managers,* 2nd ed., Upper Saddle River, NJ, and Toronto: Prentice Hall.

Fellows, C. Michael, 1997. *Economic Issues: A Canadian Perspective,* Toronto, and Irwin: McGraw-Hill Ryerson.

Flynn, Sean Masaki, 2011. *Economics for Dummies,* 2nd Edition, – Hoboken, N.J, and Indianapolis: Wiley Publishing Inc.

Pool, John Charles, 1985. *The Instant Economist.* Reading, Mass; Don Mills, ON: Addison- Wesley Publishing Co.

Riddell, Tom; Jean Shackel ford, Steve Stamos, and Goeffrey Schneider, 2008. *Economics: A Tool for Critically Understanding Society,* 8th Edition, – Boston, Toronto: Pearson Addison Wesley.

Samuelson, Paul A., (Paul Anthony), William D. Nordhaus, 2010. *Economics,* 19th ed., Boston: McGraw-Hill Irwin.

Sander, Peter, 2014. 101 *Things Everyone Should Know about Economics,* 2nd ed., Avon, MA: Adams Media.

Sowell, Thomas, 2011. *Basic Economics: a common sense guide to the economy,* 4th ed., New York: Basic Books.

Stiglitz, Joseph E., Walsh, Carl E., 2006. *Economics,* 4th ed., New York: W.W. Norton.

ABBREVIATIONS

HIV/ARV = Human Immunodeficiency Virus/Antiretro Viral Drugs-Drugs used to treat the virus that causes AIDS.
GDP –Gross Domestic Product
GNP –Gross National Product
LDAC –Least Developed African Countries
LDC –Less Developed Countries
Es –Elasticity of Supply
Ed –Elasticity of Demand
MU –Marginal Utility
LDR –Law of Diminishing Returns
TR –Total Revenue
AR –Average Revenue
TC –Total Costs
AC –Average Costs
FC –Fixed Costs
VC –Variable Costs
AVC –Average Variable Costs
MR –Marginal Revenue
MC –Marginal Cost
MRA –Marginal Revenue for sub market A
MRB –Marginal Revenue for sub market B
MRT –Sum of Marginal Revenue for the 2 sub markets
P –Price
GM –General Motors
R & D –Research and Development
MMZ –Mineral Marketing Corporation of Zimbabwe
GMB –Grain Marketing Board

DMB –Dairy Marketing Board
OPEC –Organization of Petroleum Exporting Countries
DRC –Democratic Republic of Congo
APS –Average Propensity to Save
MPS –Marginal Propensity to Save
MPC –Marginal Propensity to Consume
Yd –Total Disposable Income for a country
AMD –Aggregate Monetary Demand
G –Government expenditure
MPP –Marginal Physical Product
MRP –Marginal Revenue Product
NRZ –National Railways of Zimbabwe
ZR –Zambia Railways
ZA –Zambia Airways
ZIMCO –Zambia Industrial & Mining Corporation Ltd.
ZCCM –Zambia Consolidated Copper Mines Ltd.
RST –Roan Selection Trust Ltd.
INDECO –Industrial Corporation Ltd.
HIPC –High Indebted Per Capita Countries
MPC –Marginal Private Costs
MSC –Marginal Social Costs
MB –Marginal Benefit
CBA –Cost Benefit Analysis
FDI –Foreign Direct Investments
FI –Foreign Investment
ZMK –Zambian Kwacha
Zim$ --Zimbabwean Dollar
BoZ –Bank of Zambia
NAIRU –Non-Accelerating Inflation Rate of Unemployment
NRU –Natural Rate of Unemployment
Tazara –Tanzania Zambia Railway Line
IMF –International Monetary Fund
NAFTA –North American Free-trade Agreement
SADC –Southern African Development Countries
COMESA –Common Market for Eastern & Southern Africa
GMOs –Genetically Modified Organisms

GLOSSARY

Absolute Advantage: Term used in international trade to describe a condition when one country can produce more of a particular good with the *same amount of* resources as another country uses producing the same good. For ex., US being the best country to produce computers. That is, the ability of country A to produce a good more efficiently (a greater output per unit of input) than country B.

Aggregate Demand: The total quantity (or demand) of planned or desired spending in the economy in a given period in an economy. It is determined by the aggregate price level with influence from – government spending, net exports, domestic investments, consumption, and the money supply.

Aggregate Supply: The total value (or quantity) of goods and services that firms would willingly supply in a given period in an economy. It is determined by available inputs, technology, and the price level.

Allocative Efficiency: Is when you target allocating scarce resources for the production of goods and services that consumers most greatly desire to consume. Perfect competition leads to allocative efficiency.

Appreciation of Currency: Is the relative strengthening of a currency in a flexible exchange rate system. The appreciated currency rises in cost and value relative to the depreciated currency.

Average Propensity to Consume: Average propensity to consume (APC) is the total consumption divided by total disposable income. This is the average consumption income ratio.

Average Propensity to Save: Average propensity to save (APS) is the total saving divided by total disposable income.

Balance of Payments: A summary of record of a country's transactions that typically involves payments and receipt of foreign exchange. Credit items and debit ones must balance, since each good and service that a country buys or sells must be paid for in one way or another.

Balance of Trade: Part of a country's balance of payments that concerns with imports or exports of goods (e.g., capital goods, oil). That is, the difference between the value of exports and the value of imports of visible items (goods and services).

Barriers to Entry: These are factors that impede *entry* into a market to reduce the amount of competition or number of producers; examples may be using – tariffs, legal barriers, or government regulations.

Budget Deficit: The amount by which government expenditures exceed government revenues during the accounting period usually a year.

Business Cycles: Fluctuations in total national output, income, and employment, the up and down, expansion or contractions experienced in many sectors of the economy. The lengths of these valleys and hills could vary (e.g., 2 – 5 years).

Capital: Is interpreted as machines, lands, factories, inventories, and infrastructure used to produce output; that is the stock of a society's produced means of production.

Capitalism: This is an economy where basic resources and capital goods in society are *owned privately*. Depending on the market structure – decisions are made by individual firms, businesses or individuals; here private markets are used to allocate resources and generate incomes. Small firms rely on pure competition, while quite larger ones behave as monopolies or oligopolies. The guiding motive for firms is *profitability*, and *self-interest* or greed in case of individuals.

Cartel: Is when a group of firms or countries acts together as a single coordinated force that colludes to restrict output in order to drive up prices. This form of organization is also used to limit or eliminate competition among its members.

Command Economy: Is a *centrally planned* economy, where key economic functions of: *what, how,* and *for whom* – are mainly determined by government directives. It is similar to communism; with diluted ownership of means of production.

Communism: In economic structure such as operated in old China or former Soviet Union – the main characteristics are: socialization of labor, centralization and ownership of the means of production, and centralized coordination of production,; credit policy is also centralized and alienation or exploitation of workers is greatly reduced through government regulation.

Comparative Advantage: A theory developed by David Ricardo. In international trade, a country's productive advantage with respect to a particular commodity, based on its ability to give up *fewer* other commodities to produce a unit of the commodity than another country would have to give up. That is, a country should *specialize* in producing and exporting those commodities which it can produce at *relatively lower* cost and import those goods for which it is a *relatively high cost* producer. This relative cost of production (comparative advantage) is most significant in determining *mutually beneficial* patterns of trade among nations. If all countries followed that – total worldwide output would increase thereby raising living standards all around.

Consumer Price Index (CPI): An economic indicator compiled by Central Statistics Office (CSO) for a market basket (bundle of goods and services – among them basic necessities) used to measure changes in the prices of goods and services bought by a typical family (about 6 people). This is a weighted average composite of goods and services commonly consumed by an average family size.

Cost, Average Fixed: Total fixed cost (TFC) divided by total units of output.

Cost, Average Variable: Total variable cost (TVC) divided by total units of output.

Cost, Average: Total cost (TC) divided by the number of production units.

Cost-Push Inflation: This is a general increase in prices associated with increases in the cost of production, an upward shift of the aggregate supply curve; sometimes referred to as 'supply inflation'.

Costs, Fixed: Costs which have to be paid regardless of whether the firm is producing or not; the firm has to bear these in the short run even if out is zero.

Costs, Variable: Costs that vary with the amount of output produced; e.g., labor or resources. These fluctuate depending on the firm's activity and the productive process.

Crowding Out: Loss of funding or resources occurring as a result of competition between a country's economic units for the use of those limited resources. When government borrows from capital market for spending on its programs, it deprives businesses of necessary capital, thus, it 'crowds out'.

Debt, Government: The total obligations of a government such as bonds and short-term borrowings.

Debt, National: The net accumulation of a country's budget deficits, or the total indebtedness of a society.

Deflation: Is defined as when the overall level of prices in the economy is falling.

Demand-Pull Inflation: A general increase in prices arising from increasing excess demand for a given level of output; i.e., a major increase in aggregate demand.

Depreciation: Occurs when the economy's stocks of capital decrease caused by wear and tear or obsolescence (when an old machine or tool is no longer wanted or is outdated or replaced by new technology). That is the loss of value due to use or obsolescence. It also means the loss of value to any valuable good or commodity due to use or market forces – such as caused by currency exchange rates.

Depression: A prolonged downswing of economic activity in a society causing mass unemployment; because national output is below the potential level, there is excess capacity. A depression is usually more severe and lasts longer than a *recession.*

Devaluation: When a country's currency is revised downward, its value pegged in terms of a foreign currency such as dollar, falls.

Diminishing Marginal Utility, Law of: This states that – as more and more of any one commodity is consumed, its marginal utility declines.

Diminishing Returns: That is when each additional unit of a resource (input) used in production process brings forth successively *smaller* amounts of output. As more units of a variable input, such as labor are added to a fixed quantity of other factors of production, the amount that each *additional unit* of this variable factor adds to the total output will eventually begin to diminish.

Disinflation: The process of reducing a high (or hyper) inflation rate. Zimbabwe could do with disinflation period.

Disposable Income: Is basically the take - home pay or that part of total national income available to households for consumption or saving.

Dumping: Sale by an exporting nation of its product at a *lower price* in an importing country than in its own country. This tends to ruin the importer's domestic industry but strengthening the exporter's market share. This may be a deliberate policy.

Duopoly: A market structure where there are only two sellers.

efficiency.

Elastic Demand, (Price-elastic demand): When price elasticity of demand exceeds 1 in absolute value, it means that the percent change in quantity *demanded* is greater than the percent change in price.

Elasticity: This is a term used by economists to denote the responsiveness of one variable to changes in another. It is the sensitivity of demand or supply of a good to changes in its price; it equals the percent change in quantity demanded (or supplied) by the percent change in price. For example – the elasticity of good A with respect to good B means the percent change in A for every one percent change in B.

Employment, Seasonal: Unemployment or joblessness created as a result of seasonal variations or demand for labor.

Equilibrium: Is term used to denote the state in which an economic entity is *at rest* or in which the forces operation on the entity (e.g. demand or supply) are in balance so that there is no tendency for change. Otherwise any change causes disequilibrium.

Exchange Rate: The price of a country's currency in terms of another country's currency.

Externality: That is a cost or benefit that falls not on the person (s) of firm (s) directly involved in an activity but on others; so-called third-party effect (such as cross border acid rain). This causer or source of it is not obliged to bear it. The costs are usually borne by the public in form of 'social costs'. Externality can be either positive or beneficial (benefits), negative or detrimental (external costs).

Factors of Production: Inputs which go into the production process such as – labor, land, and capital. They are the resources needed to produce goods and services.

Fiscal Policy: Government policy concerned with the tax and expenditure activities. To balance or unbalance the budget, government either increases its spending and/or it lowers tax rates. This policy is designed to promote/fight certain macroeconomic objectives – full employment, stable prices, economic growth, and balance-of-payments equilibrium. Government uses it to cure recessions or simply to boost economic activity.

Foreign Exchange Rate: The rate or price, at which one country's currency is exchanged for the currency of another country. For example – how much would 1 Zimbabwean dollar fetch in terms of Zambian Kwachas. A *fixed exchange rate* is when a country pegs its currency at a given exchange rate and be ready to stand by that rate. *Flexible exchange rates* are those determined by market supply and demand forces; also referred to as *floating exchange rates.*

Free Trade: A situation in which all commodities can be freely imported or exported without special taxes or restrictions being levied.

Gross Domestic Product (GDP): This is the market value of all goods and services produced in an economy using factors of production located within the country, in a given period of time; such as per quarter or per year. This sum (Y) is composed of all expenditures on consumption (C), investments (I), government purchases (G), and exports (EX), less (minus) expenditures on imports (IM). Or Y = C + I + G + EX – IM.

Gross National Product (GNP): The market value of all final goods and services produced in a given accounting period by factors of production *owned* by citizens of that country.

Human Capital: Is the knowledge and skills that the people of a country can use to help them produce output. The higher the quality of human capital, the higher the nation's output. Sweden's 8 million people, produces bugger output than many countries in Latin America or Africa combined where population is twentyfold.

Hyperinflation: Is inflation at extremely high rates (at f.ex., 100, 1000, 1 million, or even 1 billion percent a year). In Western countries any rate of inflation in excess of 20 or 30 percent is considered hyper. In recent times Zimbabwe experienced a period of hyperinflation; in such a situation, to buy a loaf of bread one needs a suitcase of money.22 *Galloping inflation*, is high but within hundreds' limit per year; a situation common in many African countries. Although Zambia's inflation rate is now a single digit (6-9% currently), it had to be contained from over 50%.

in its export prices – is a positive or improvement in a country's terms of trade; and deterioration in its terms of trade means a relative increase in its import prices.

Income Elasticity of Demand: Since the demand for any given product does not only depend on the product's price but also the buyer's income – it measures this responsiveness. Thus, it is the percent change in quantity demanded divided by the percent change in income. It measures how much the *demand* for a product changes when income changes.

Inefficiency in Resource Allocation: This is a condition in a noncompetitive market in which the good's price *does not equal* marginal cost (MC).

Inelastic Demand, (Price-inelastic demand): When price elasticity of demand is below 1 in absolute value, it signifies that the percent change in quantity *demanded* is less than the percent change in price. So, when price declines, total revenue (TR) also declines; and when the price is increased, TR also goes up.

Infant Industry: A new industry which has been recently established in a country and has had no time to establish itself to exploit possible economies of scale or other efficiencies. In developing countries, tariffs are normally used to protect these industries.

Inflation: Is when the overall level of prices in the economy is rising; expressed as the percent of annual increase in general price level. Also it is also defined by some index such as CPI, wholesale price index, or GDP price deflator.

Interest Rate: The price or cost of borrowing money. It is sometimes expressed as the rate of return to owners of financial capital.

Inventories: Stocks of goods kept on hand to meet orders from other producers and customers.

Investment: Spending by government or firms to increase the economy's stock of capital as well as the value of any increases in the inventories.

Invisible Hand: This term was coined by Adam Smith to suggest that individuals who are motivated *only* by private (not social) interest will nevertheless be guided *invisibly* by the market to take actions and decisions beneficial to the welfare of society. In other words, when firms are constrained by competition, each firm's greed causes it to act in a socially optimal way, as if guided by an invisible hand.

Keynesian Economics: Named after its original advocate – John Maynard Keynes; who advances an argument for greater participation of government in the economy. The emphasis is on macroeconomic variables, with a special role of *aggregate expenditure* in determining national income and unemployment equilibrium. Real and monetary analysis is combined with fiscal policy as a cure for weak economy. Keynes observed that left alone market forces cannot lead toward full employment equilibrium.

Laissez-faíre: A doctrine demanding that the state should largely leave the economy on its own devices. 'Do not interfere' as Adam Smith counseled. That the role of government should only be limited to maintenance of law and order; and the production of public goods such as – roads, education, health, etc..

Law of Demand: Is a principle concerning the relationship between price and quantity *demanded*; the lower the price, the higher the quantity of a commodity demanded *ceteris paribus* (all other things held constant). Thus, price and quantity demanded are *inversely* related.

Law of Supply: Is an economic theory which stipulates that – the lower the price, the lower the quantity supplied, *ceteris paribus* (all other variables held constant). Thus, the price and quantity of a commodity *supplied* are positively related.

Long-Run Shutdown Condition: When the firm's total revenues (TR) exceed its *variable costs* (VC) but are *less than* its total costs (TC); the firm will continue operating until when its fixed costs (FC) contracts (say for buildings) expire in the long-run.

Macroeconomics: A branch of economics concerned with large economic aggregates such as GDP, total employment, overall price level, and how these aggregates are determined.

Marginal Cost: Is how much total costs increase when you produce *one more unit* of output. That is the change in total cost (TC) resulting from raising the rate of production by one unit.

Marginal Propensity to Consume: The change in consumption divided by the change in income; MPC = $\Delta C/\Delta Y$.

Marginal Propensity to Save: The change in saving divided by the change in income that brought it about; MPS = $\Delta S/\Delta Y$.

Marginal Revenue: The change in a firm's total revenue (TR) arising from the sale of one additional unit.

Marginal Utility: The additional or extra satisfaction yielded from consuming one *additional unit* of a commodity, with amounts of all other goods consumed held constant.

Market Economy: This is an economy where the *private decisions* of consumers, resource suppliers, and firms (or companies) determine how resources are allocated, with very limited interventions (to ensure fair play) from the government. It depends on market forces (i.e. supply and demand). Some refer to it as a laissez-faire (left alone) economic system.

Market Failures: The situations when the economy or markets deliver non-optimal social outcomes. i.e., the inability of the markets to produce an efficient (or acceptable) outcomes. Some common causes of market failure are – asymmetric information (partial, deceitful, or misleading information), monopoly, externalities, and public goods.

Microeconomics: A branch of economics which deals with the interrelationships of individual businesses, firms, industries, consumers or households, and other factors of production made up in an economy. It pays particular attention to markets.

Mixed Economy: In this economy, public and private sectors are quite substantial. The role of the market and private enterprise are significant determining factors. The state also plays an important role in as far as variables like – full employment business regulations are concerned.

Monetary Policy: Government policy concerned with the supply of money and credit in the economy and the manipulation of the rate of interest to stimulate or slow down economic activity; usually administered by the Central Bank. The macroeconomic objectives it tries to achieve are same as for fiscal policy – full employment, stable prices, economic growth, and balance of payment equilibrium.

Monopoly: A market structure in which a commodity, which has no close substitutes, is supplied by a single firm.

Monopsony: A mirror image of monopoly. That is a market in which there is a *single buyer*; a buyer's monopoly.

Multinational Corporation (MNC): One which operates within more than one country.

Natural Monopoly: A firm or industry where average cost per unit of production falls sharply over the entire range of its output; e.g. local electricity distribution; an industry characterized by one large producer producing output at a much lower cost (more efficiently) than many small producers. Because of that advantage, it *undersells* its rivals and ends up being the only surviving firm in the industry.

Nominal Interest Rates: Interest rates measuring the returns to a loan in terms of money borrowed and money returned (contrasted to *real interest rates*).

Nominal Prices: Is the price as it is actually observed in current dollars (or which ever currency is being used); this is contrasted with *real prices,* which is adjusted for inflation.

Oligopoly: A situation of imperfect competition where an industry is determined by a small number of suppliers; these few firms can collude or form a cartel to reduce output and drive up profits the way a monopoly does. Because some firms produce undifferentiated product and others a differentiated one – there is recognition of interdependence.

Opportunity Cost: This is the cost of a good or service as measured in terms of the *alternative* good or

Paradigms: In a specific discipline such as – Marxian Economics, Institutional or Orthodox Economics; there is a set of concepts, values, assumptions, and practices which are relied on during a particular period of time.

Per Capita Income: Total national income divided by total population of a nation. It is a measure of how well-off people of a society are in comparison to others.

Perfect Competition: A market structure where there is a large number of small firms producing and selling a *homogeneous product* in a competitive market with no barrier to entry or exit; no firm or consumer is large enough to affect the market price.

Present Value: The value today of a sum to be received or paid in the future, adjusted by a prevailing or assumed interest rate.

Price Ceiling: A market intervention where the government ensures that the price of a good or service, *stays below* the free market (equilibrium) price.

Price Discrimination: When the same product is sold to different consumers at different prices.

Price Elasticity of Demand: The sensitivity of demand for a product *to changes* in its price.

Price Elasticity of Supply: The sensitivity of supply of a product *to changes* in its price.

Price Floor: A market intervention where the government keeps the price of a good or service *above* its free-market price.

Prisoner's Dilemma: This is a tricky situation where a pair of prisoners (or firms) has to decide whether to cooperate or not. The dilemma is that – although the individual incentives favor an option of not cooperating, but both players would in fact be *better off* if they could find a way to cooperate.

Product Differentiation: Creating distinctive features, characteristics, or differences to substitute products as a form of business strategy. These differences can be in form of brand names, coloring, packaging, or even through advertising. These characteristics make similar products less-than-perfect substitutes.

Production Possibilities Curve: Is a graph which illustrates *scarcity* and *opportunity cost* by showing that any combination a society chooses – to have more of one type of good implies a sacrifice of some other type of good.

Productively Efficient: That is producing a good or service at the least (lowest) possible cost.

Property Rights: Where productive property is privately owned such as in capitalism – the owner's rights to control the use of these productive resources are the property rights.

Quantity Theory of Money: The theory that the overall level of prices in the economy is proportional to the quantity of money circulating in the economy.

Rational Expectations Hypothesis: This holds that – people make unbiased forecasts and that; people use all available information and economic theory or principles when making these forecasts. This implies that – people will *optimally change* their behavior in response to policy changes. Inversely, depending on a situation – their behavioral changes can greatly limit the effectiveness of the policy changes.

Real Interest Rates: These are interest rates taking into account compensation *for inflation* by measuring the returns to a loan in terms of units of money lent and units of money returned (contrasted to *nominal interest rates*).

Real Prices: Measures how much of one kind of thing (e.g. hours worked) one has to give up in return for another good or service, no matter what happens to nominal prices.

Real Wages: This is when nominal wages are adjusted for inflation; that is, wages measured not in terms of current dollars – which is what *nominal or money wages* are; but rather in terms of how much output can be purchased with these current dollars. If wages are raised by 5% and the rate of inflation also increases by 5% - in that case the *real wage* remains the same.

Recession: The time during which an economy's total output falls. The economic activity slows down causing unemployment and excess capacity. In USA when GDP declines for two successive quarters in a year, this is regarded as recession.

Resource Allocation: The way in which the economy distributes its resources (the inputs) among potential uses so as to produce a particular set of commodities.

Savings: Is all the income earned by households and not spent on consuming goods and services.

service *one must forego* to secure it. The value of the best foregone alternative option; what you would lose or give up in order to pursue a particular option. How much would one lose by opening up a private tutoring school versus to simply sell/offer ones' services as a teacher?

Short-Run Shutdown Condition: This is a situation when a firm's total revenues (TR) are *less than* its variable costs (VC) and the firm is *better off* shutting down immediately because then they would only lose its fixed costs (FC).

Stagflation: This term describes the coexistence of unemployment (which is stagnation) and inflation in a country. For a longtime Zimbabwe was experiencing 'stagflation'.

Sticky Prices: These are prices which are slow to adjust to shocks; the price stickiness is undesirable sometimes because it can cause recession to linger around.

Stock: Are shares of ownership in a corporation or firm. These may be common stock and/or preferred stock.

Substitutes: Goods that compete with each other; Pepsi and Coca-Cola are classical examples. Contrast this with complements goods which go together, e.g., left and right shoes.

Supply-Shock Inflation: Inflation associated with the supply side of markets normally due to a sharp increase in costs.

Supply-Side Economics: Putting emphasis on policy measures intended to affect aggregate supply or potential output. Is also referred to as *Reaganomics.*

Terms of Trade: Expresses the prices of a country's exports in relation to its imports. A relative increase

Trade Barriers: Protectionist devices a country can use to discourage imports; for ex., tariffs, quotas, and nontariff barriers (NTBs) the regulations or protocols.

Unemployment Rate: Measures the number of employable people unemployed, expressed as a percentage of the total number of people in the labor force. This is not a useful tool in most sub-Saharan countries where only a small fraction of the population can find formal jobs.

Unemployment, Cyclical: This arises from changes in the demand for labor during the business cycle.

Unemployment, Frictional: Is unemployment arising from workers changing jobs, etc.; workers may move to better paid jobs with better conditions, or due to acquisition of new skills or training.

Unemployment, Hidden: In any labor market, you may have workers (individuals), who due to some reason or frustration have given up looking for a job.

Unemployment, Structural: Permanent unemployment as a result of shifting product demand and/or technological changes, necessitating workers to require new skills or re-training. This impacts job skill mobility.

Utility: This is a concept economists use to measure peoples' happiness when they compare all possible things that they may experience. By how much does one prefer fish to chicken at a particular time, in a particular situation, given x-amount of dollars.

Value Added: This is the value of a final product less the cost of production.

ABOUT THE AUTHORS

KAELA B MULENGA:
PhD, MSC., MA., BS.

Educator, Researcher, Blogger.

Swedish Institute Scholar, Uppsala, Sweden; Fulbright Scholar/Visiting Professor – Kentucky University, Lexington, KY, USA; Kansas State University, Manhattan, KS, USA.

Associate BS Agric., University of Connecticut, Storrs, CONN, USA; MS, Development Economics – Swedish Agricultural University, Uppsala, Sweden; Business Studies – Uppsala University; Economic History, Stockholm University, Stockholm, Sweden; Research Associate – The Nordic Africa Institute, Uppsala, Sweden; English Literature – George Town University, Washington, D.C., USA.

Upon returning from the US, the author held several senior civil service positions with GRZ, among them as Assistant/Under Secretary in the Ministry of Rural Development. He participated in the planning, drawing up and implementation of 1st, 2nd, and 3rd Zambia National Development Plans.

After nationalization of Zambia's economy by President Kenneth Kaunda, the author held several portfolios within INDECO/ZIMCO corporate structure.

Later the author left for further studies in Scandinavia. After that he came back and took a teaching position at the University of Zambia (UNZA) – Faculty of Agricultural Sciences (Senior Lecturer). Teaching and research interests have covered: micro & macro economics, development economics, political science, statistics, environmental science & agricultural economics.

In Canada, while working as a full time as Analyst Socio-Economic Issues at Federal Statistics Canada, the author undertook session teaching assignments at University of Toronto.

The author is widely published and most of the material is readily available through the internet.

K.B. Mulenga and F.L. Mupakati, have been associates in Toronto, Canada for a long time. Similarity in interests goes all the way back to colonial era when, at one time – Zambia (formerly Northern Rhodesia) and Zimbabwe (formerly Southern Rhodesia & Rhodesia) were part of one country called: Federation of Rhodesia & Nyasaland. Malawi being the other country.

FRANCIS L MUPAKATI:
BA (Hons), MA (Econ).

Frank L Mupakati, BA (Hons) Econ. University of Kent at Canterbury. UK, MA (Econ). Lakehead University, Ont. Canada.

When the author was a lecturer at the University of Zimbabwe, he observed that many students, particularly those preparing to sit for A-Levels had weak knowledge in economics basics. To remedy this, he came up with a **Study Aids Compendium**, which later was published as *"Focus on A-Level Economics with Model Answers"* in 1990.

The usefulness of this material was tested with his students at: Harare Polytechnic, Churchill High School and at the University of Zimbabwe Evening School.

In late 90s, as politics of president Robert Mugabe became unattainable, Francis L Mupakati moved to Canada. In Canada he had a stellar career - at management level, with Canadian Banks. He left the Banking Industry to start up his own small business.

Up to his passing on (Spring 2017) – Francis was working on theories related to: *probability and prediction.* His goal was to eventually develop *soft ware* which could have applications in gambling – such as a tool for lottery plays.

******

Printed in the United States
By Bookmasters